STRATEGIC PRAYER

Rev. Dr. Caesar O. Benedo

This book was formerly published as part of "Understanding the Art of Prayer."

Copyright © 2015 by Caesar Benedo

STRATEGIC PRAYER

Copyright © 2017 by Caesar Benedo

ISBN-13: 978-99919-71-92-6

All right reserved. No part of this publication may be reproduced, stored in a retrieval system, or transmitted in any form or by any means - electronic, mechanical, photocopying, recording, scanning or otherwise-except for brief quotations in critical reviews or articles, without the prior permission of the copyright holder.

Note: personal pronouns for God, Jesus and the Holy Spirit are lowercased in keeping with the different Bible versions used in this book.

Scripture quotations marked KJV are taken from the Authorized King James version © 1991 by World Bible Publishers, Inc.

Scripture quotations marked NIV are taken from the New International version © 1973, 1978, 1984 by the International Bible Society

Scripture quotations marked NKJV are taken from the New King James version © 1982 by Thomas Nelson, Inc.

Scripture quotations marked NASB are taken from the New America Standard Bible © 1960, 1962, 1963, 1968, 1971, 1972, 1973, 1975, 1977, 1995 by The Lockman Foundation

Scripture quotations marked NLT are taken from the Holy Bible, New Living Translation ®, copyright © 1996, 2004 by Tyndale Charitable Trust. Used by permission of Tyndale House Publishers. All rights reserved.

Scripture quotations marked ESV are taken from the Holy Bible, English Standard Version Copyright © 2001 by Crossway Bibles, a division of Good News Publishers

Scripture quotations marked AMP are taken from the Amplified Bible © 1954, 1958, 1962, 1964, 1965, 1987 by The Lockman Foundation

Scripture quotations marked THE MESSAGE are taken from THE MESSAGE: The Bible in Contemporary Language © 2002 by Eugene H. Peterson. All rights reserved.

Scripture quotations marked HCSB are taken from the Holman Christian Standard Bible © 1999, 2000, 2002, 2003 by Holman Bible Publishers, Nashville Tennessee.

Scripture quotations marked RSV are taken from the Revised Standard Version of the Bible copyright © 1946, 1952, and 1971 the Division of Christian Education of the National Council of the Churches of Christ in the United States of America. Used by permission. All rights reserved.

ACKNOWLEDGEMENT

A special thanks to the following people for their love, support and prayer to make this book a reality. Mr. and Mrs. Ononiwu, Mr. and Mrs. Ugwulor, Mrs. Sheyi Bonou, Pastor Fadel Akpiti, Mr. Samuel Fabrice Yomo, Pastor Samuel Kalu, Mr. and Mrs. Odjo, Mr. Kingsley Eme, Mr. and Mrs. Fajemirokun, Mrs. Vivian Asempapa, Mrs. Georgette Gbesset Baffoh, Pastor Veronica Bampoe-Darko, Pastor Maximo Deleon, Rev. Emenike Paul Ezechiluo, Rev. Lucile Sossou, Prophet Holy Joy, Rev. Dr. Nicaise Laleye, Rev. Alphonse Dagnonnoueton, Rev. and Pastor Mrs. Tigo, Rev. Isidore Godonou, Rev. and Mrs. Oluwaseyitan, Rev. Mrs. and Bishop Meshack Okonkwo etc.

A million thanks to the members of my family for your love, encouragement, care, and support. May God richly bless you all.

I want to use this opportunity to express my appreciation to Pastor Benjamin Opeyemi Olaosebikan, and Pastor Eric Osei Yaw for their brotherly support, encouragement, and prayer.

A special thanks to Bishop Kwesi Adutwum for your love, encouragement, advice, support, and prayer. I'm indeed thankful to God for your life and for the incredible support you gave me. May God richly bless you.

A special thanks to Rev. Mrs Betty N. Coleman for your love, encouragement, support and prayer. May God richly bless and reward you for the great work you are doing for the kingdom.

I want to use this opportunity to express my gratitude to Pastor Zina Pierre for your love, support and prayer. May the Lord continue to bless you.

A special thanks to my Bishop, James Nana Ofori Attah for your love, encouragement, support and prayer. May the Lord continue to bless you.

I want to use this opportunity to express my gratitude to Apostle Michael Adeyemi Adefarasin for bringing out the best in me. I admire your commitment to excellence, your sincere desire to make a difference and your love for good work.

A special thanks to my papa, the archbishop Nicholas Duncan-Williams (founder of Action Chapel International), for your prayers, leadership, and spiritual guidance. May God continue to use you to raise and empower men and women to fulfil their divine purpose.

Words cannot convey how much I appreciate the love, care, support and prayer of senior deacon, and mama Georgina Lamptey for all the investment both of you made in my life. Thank you for standing by me at the very moment I needed it the most. May the Lord richly bless you.

DEDICATION

I dedicate this book to everyone who desires to take his or her prayer life to the advanced levels and dimensions of prayer, and produce better results.

Table of Contents

ACKNOWLEDGEMENT III
DEDICATION V
PRAYER 1
INTRODUCTION 3

Chapter One   INTRODUCTION TO INTERCESSION 7

Important Points 7
Ministry of Intercession 9
Intercession Strategy 11
Importance of Intercession 19
How to Intercede 22
Role of Intercessor 24

Chapter Two   GUIDES TO SPIRITUAL WARFARE 27

Art of Spiritual Warfare 30
Spiritual Warfare Strategy 34
Levels of Spiritual Warfare 42
Role of a Prayer Warrior 54
Importance of Spiritual Warfare 55
Weapons of Spiritual Warfare 56

Chapter Three   WIELDING THE SWORD 59

Chapter Four   BATTLE OF THE MIND 67

Chapter Five   SPIRITUAL MAPPING 79

Chapter Six   SATAN'S SCHEMES AND BATTLE STRATEGY 85

Chapter Seven   BREAKING DEMONIC ALTARS 93

Chapter Eight BREAKING TRANSGENERATIONAL CURSES.101

Chapter Nine   PATTERNS OF THE BLOODLINE 109

Chapter Ten   HOUSEHOLD ENEMY 125

Chapter Eleven   BINDING THE STRONG MAN 131

Chapter Twelve   DESTROYING DEMONIC ARROWS 137

Chapter Thirteen   ENFORCING PROPHETIC DECREES 147

Chapter Fourteen   GROANING IN THE SPIRIT 157

IMPORTANT ABBREVIATIONS 163

PRAYER OF SALVATION 165

PRAYER

Heavenly Father, in agreement with the Scripture that says the entrance of your word gives light and understanding to the simple (Ps.119:130), I beseech you to enlighten the eyes of my heart that I may understand the mystery of prayer as I read this book. Grant me insight and the grace to take hold of the truth, just as you did for Lydia in Acts16:14, when you opened her heart to receive the truth spoken by the apostle Paul about your Son Jesus.

By the power of the Holy Spirit, I pull down every imagination, argument and thought that does not conform to biblical truths, concepts and principles that the wicked may want to use to hinder me from accepting the truth in this book. It is written that I shall know the truth, and the truth will set me free (Jn.8:32).

Dear Lord, open my eyes to the truth in this book and deliver me from the spirit of error in Jesus name. Amen!

I urge, then, first of all, that requests, prayers, intercession and thanksgiving be made for everyone— for kings and all those in authority, that we may live peaceful and quiet lives in all godliness and holiness. This is good, and pleases God our Savior, who wants all men to be saved and to come to a knowledge of the truth. For there is one God and one mediator between God and men, the man Christ Jesus.

(1 Tim. 2:1-5 NIV)

INTRODUCTION

According to the Bible, there are different kinds of prayers (1 Tim.2:1). For the benefit of this teaching, I would focus on strategic prayer. This type of prayer requires some level of knowledge and skill to produce the intended results. The knowledge and understanding needed for this prayer can be acquired through study, practice and observation.

Some dictionaries define strategy as a plan for achieving a particular long-term goal. *Cambridge Advanced Learner's Dictionary* defines it as "a detailed plan for achieving success in situations such as war, politics, business, industry or sport, or the skill of planning for such situations."

There are basically two types of strategic prayers: defensive, known as intercession, and offensive, called warfare. The first is a ministry, while the latter is an art. They also differs from each other in the rules of engagement, strategy, characteristics, roles, etc. However, both require minimum expertise to produce the intended results.

STRATEGIC PRAYER

People always confuse both prayers by using them interchangeably, because they think intercession and warfare are the same. The truth is they are not, and unless there is a proper understanding of this fact, we cannot be very effective in these two branches of strategic prayer, no matter how much we try.

Intercession and warfare is like boxing and wrestling, which are both combat sports but differ in the rules of the game. You have to understand the rules and play by them to win in boxing, while in wrestling anything is allowed, provided you don't break the neck of your opponent. You will be disqualified when you break the rules in boxing, but you can defeat your opponent either by tricks or skills in wrestling.

Just as boxing differs from wrestling in the rules, condition, style, timing, fighting tools, and so on, though they are both combat sports, intercession and spiritual warfare also have similarities and differences (similarities because they are both strategic prayers; differences in the rules, strategy, tactics, fighting tools, or weapons).

Understanding the ministry of intercession and the art of spiritual warfare is a major key to a consistent prayer life. Those who master the art of prayer understand the main differences and similarities between intercession and warfare. As earlier said, the first is a ministry, while the second is an art. *Merriam-Webster* includes in its definition of ministry the following, "The office, duties, or work of a religious minister." *Concise Oxford Dictionary* – Tenth edition, also includes the following in its definition of an art, "A skill at doing a specific thing."

INTRODUCTION

Any church without a balanced teaching on these two branches of strategic prayer cannot be very effective in the area of prayer.

I have seen a lot of people who claim to be Intercessors, but when you take a closer look at how they pray, and listen to what they say during prayer, you can't help asking whether they really understand what intercession means. Claiming to be one doesn't make any difference — what matters is the understanding you have about the ministry of intercession and the grace to intercede (the call to be an Intercessor, according to one of my friends).

There are many famous Intercessors and prayer Warriors who have done great exploits through the ministry of prayer, with so many fruits they could point to, who need to provide some materials through writing for training the younger generation who greatly desires to walk their path. Many start prayer ministry without the proper foundation and understanding of the art, focusing only on the fruits of others with the assumption that if it works for Mr. A, it will work for them (which is a fatal assumption).

And he told this parable: "A man had a fig tree planted in his vineyard, and he came seeking fruit on it and found none. And he said to the vinedresser, 'Look, for three years now I have come seeking fruit on this fig tree, and I find none. Cut it down. Why should it use up the ground?' And he answered him, 'Sir, let it alone this year also, until I dig around it and put on manure. Then if it should bear fruit next year, well and good; but if not, you can cut it down.'"

(Lk. 13:6-9 ESV)

CHAPTER 1

INTRODUCTION TO INTERCESSION

The Lord Jesus told a parable in Luke 13:6-9 that gives us insight to the ministry of intercession. The story illustrates the role and importance of intercession. It talks about a man who planted a fig tree in his garden, and he came seeking fruit on it for three years but found none.

Finally, he asked the gardener to cut the tree down because it wasn't producing fruit but kept using the nutrients from the soil. The gardener stood between the tree and its owner, plead its case, stopped the judgment, and secured a second chance for the tree by giving the owner some valid reasons to suspend his decision.

IMPORTANT POINTS

1. God's purpose is primary over everything else: the primary reason the land owner planted the fig tree was for it to bear fruit. This was his purpose for the tree.

STRATEGIC PRAYER

Nothing is more important to him than seeing the tree fulfilling its mandate (Prov. 19:21). Knowing your divine purpose releases your full potential and helps you to lead a happy and fulfilled life. Discover your purpose, fulfill it, and live life to the fullest! You have an assignment!

2. There is a time for everything: he waited for three whole years to get some fruit but got nothing. There is time for everything, and a season for every purpose under the sun, says the Teacher (Ecl.3:1). Time is precious! Use it wisely.

3. No good investor wants to waste time and resources: the landowner decided to cut down the fig tree because it wasn't fulfilling its purpose (producing fruit), but kept wasting his time and using the nutrients from the soil (wasting the resources). The worst thing that could happen to a person is to waste his time, resources, and life without fulfilling his purpose. How are you fulfilling your divine assignment?

The gardener was a voice, defender, mediator, an advocate, and an intercessor for the fig tree. He did for the tree what it couldn't do by itself and did not use the thing against it. This is the essence of intercessory ministry. To plead the case, defend, rescue, deliver, liberate, and protect people in prayer.

The gardener took a defensive and protective position for the fig tree against the aggression of its owner. He used his defensive skills to stop the owner from destroying the tree, despite the fact that it deserved to be cut down for wasting the owner's time, resources, and not bearing fruit. His expertise and passion gave him an advantage in intercession to overturn the death sentence pronounced against the tree. This is what I call intercession strategy (I'll expand on this as we proceed).

INTRODUCTION TO INTERCESSION

MINISTRY OF INTERCESSION

Intercession is when you use your influence to make someone in authority forgive someone else or save them from punishment (*Cambridge Advanced Learner's Dictionary*).

Intercession can be broken down into two words, inter and cession. *Merriam-Webster's Dictionary* includes in its definition of the prefix "inter-" the following: between, among, together, involving two or more. It defines "cession" as the act of giving up something (such as power, land, or rights) to another person, group, or country.

The ministry of intercession is about defending and protecting lives and destinies through prayer, by building up the wall and standing in the gap before God on behalf of the people to move his hand and release his favor on them. It gives voice to the voiceless, protection to the defenseless, liberty to those in bondage, deliverance to the afflicted, help to the needy, and so on.

Intercession places the needs and interests of others above personal desire. It is a selfless prayer characterized by passion and sincere love for the wellbeing of others. The hallmark of intercessory prayer is birthing the will and counsel of God and bringing humans into alignment with the divine agenda of God for their lives. It begins with the knowledge and understanding of God's will for mankind as revealed in the written word of God (the Holy Bible).

1 Timothy 2:5-6 says there is one God and one mediator between God and mankind, the man Christ Jesus, who gave himself as a ransom for all.

STRATEGIC PRAYER

Romans 8:34 declares Christ Jesus is at the right hand of God making intercession for us. In Hebrews 7:25, scripture states that Christ is able to save completely those who come to God through him, because he lives forever to intercede for them.

The role of Christ as the high priest over the house of God (heaven) is intercession. He mediates, defends, and protects humans in the courtroom of heaven. 1 John 2:1 calls him the advocate who pleads our case before the Father when we sin. Christ's intercessory ministry in the courtroom of heaven is to defend, protect, and plead the cause of mankind before the Godhead. He silences the voice of the wicked, covers up our weaknesses, failures, and sins, justifies us, and causes the Father to show us mercy. Without the intercessory ministry of Christ in the heavenly courtroom for humanity, the wrath of God would be poured out on mankind.

Romans 8:26-27 declares the Holy Spirit helps us in our weakness, by interceding for us according to the will of God with groaning that cannot be expressed in words, for we don't know what we ought to pray for. The spirit is willing but the body is weak, says the Lord Jesus (Matt.26:41). For this reason, the Holy Spirit helps us in our weakness by defending and protecting us before the Father, using words that are in harmony with his will.

It is written in 1 Corinthians 2:11 that no one knows the thoughts of God except the Spirit of God. Thus, the Holy Spirit uses the knowledge he has about God's plan to help our weakness and to plead our cause with spiritual words that agree with his agenda for our lives.

INTRODUCTION TO INTERCESSION

It's amazing to know that the Lord Jesus and the Holy Spirit are both in the ministry of intercession for humanity. A friend once asked, "Why should we pray, when the Lord Jesus and the Holy Spirit are both interceding for us? The intercession of the Lord Jesus and the Holy Spirit give us advantages in the courtroom of heaven.

Jesus the Son of man is our advocate in the heavenly courtroom, who pleads our cause before the Godhead and his counsel of elders. The Holy Spirit gives us utterance to articulate words in the heavenly language that no human intelligent can comprehend. Our prayers give God permission to interfere in human affairs

An intercessor is someone who stands between God and humans to defend their cause before heaven and protect them against demonic aggression. He is a mediator, defender, negotiator, advocate, etc. who seeks, defends, and protects the interests of those for whom he stands. This person is someone who understands the rules of engagement, biblical truths, concepts, and principles (i.e. the word of God), the wiles of the wicked, intercession strategy, and the ministry of intercession.

INTERCESSION STRATEGY

Intercession strategy is the expertise required for a successful defensive prayer. It is a skill that is taught, learned, and practiced by all successful intercessors. This strategy is a game plan based on biblical truths, concepts, and principles that give you an advantage in prayer. It is using scripture to build your case in a way that allows you to win when interceding.

STRATEGIC PRAYER

God does nothing outside his word, and every event in the Bible illustrates a divine truth, reveals a concept, or highlights a principle that sets a precedent for evaluating similar or related issues. Your knowledge, understanding, and application of scripture determine how well you use this strategy. The right use of this strategy gives you the upper hand over your enemies in prayer.

This game plan is your ability to spiritually diagnose an issue, discern the root cause, and deploy the appropriate weapon based on the word of God to deal with it (every situation is different from the other). An intercessor is a strategist, an expert in taking defensive measures against aggression, affliction, calamity, wickedness, and so on.

Going back to the parable of the Fig tree, the gardener was an expert in matters relating to plants or gardens. He knows when a tree bears fruit and the possible causes of infertility among trees. It is said that a fig tree bears fruit within one or two years. He understands the owner's concern and reason for wanting the tree cut down, since the required amount of time for it to produce was one to two years, and having waited three years, the tree deserved to die.

Knowing the possible causes and solution to the problem of the tree, he took a defensive measure to protect the tree from being cut down by addressing the root cause, and suggesting a possible solution based on his knowledge and experience in the field. This caused the owner to give up whatever he had against the tree, abort his plan to cut it down, and grant the tree another chance to live and produce fruit. His maneuver or tactical move based on knowledge, understanding, and experience overturned the death sentence pronounced against the tree, gave it another chance to bear fruit, and extended its life.

INTRODUCTION TO INTERCESSION

Isaiah 43:26 says put me in remembrance; let us argue the matter together, state your case that you may be acquitted. Scriptures cannot be broken. God honors his word and does whatever he says. His promises are yes and amen.

The main secret and concern of the land owner (bitterness, anger, disappointment and the decision to cut the tree down) and the tree (unfruitfulness, a waste of time and resources, the death sentence), were both unveiled to the gardener when he stood in the gap.

Intercession gives you access to top secrets, revelation knowledge, power, and authority. His maturity made him use the information he received to devise a strategy for defending the tree in order to avert the impending judgment. When he received the revelation knowledge, he did not tell it to anyone else, but used it to build a defensive case that saved the tree from death. Discretion is very crucial in the ministry of intercession. God will reveal deep secrets to you only when you are discreet (you must be trustworthy to succeed in this ministry).

Genesis 18:17-33 describes how father Abraham used this same game plan to defend the cause of Sodom and Gomorrah before God. As soon as the Lord told him that the outcry against Sodom and Gomorrah because of their sin was so great, he took a very strong defensive stand on behalf of the people and pleaded with God to stop the imminent destruction of the land.

Since father Abraham knew that God is just in his righteousness and righteous in his justice (Ps. 89:14), he asked, "Will you destroy the righteous with the wicked?

STRATEGIC PRAYER

Suppose you find fifty righteous people living in the city, will you not spare the land because of them? Surely you wouldn't do such a thing, to kill the righteous with the wicked, treating the righteous and the wicked exactly the same. Far be it from you! Will not the judge of the earth do right?" God replied, "If I find fifty righteous in the city, I will spare the whole land for their sake."

There is no doubt father Abraham was a good defense attorney who truly understood intercession strategy. Knowing the nature of God, that he would not treat the righteous and the wicked the same, and knowing his manifold wisdom in rendering justice, he took advantage of it and wisely reminded God how unlawful it is for him to destroy the righteous with the wicked. He also pointed out to God, in an attempt to protect Sodom, that killing the righteous with the wicked would not be a noble act as the righteous judge of the whole earth.

For God to prove his steadfastness and integrity, he agreed to abort the plan to destroy the land if he found in Sodom the number of righteous people father Abraham mentioned. Knowing this was a key factor he could use in his defense of Sodom, father Abraham took advantage of it and started bargaining for God to spare the land for the sake of few righteous people.

Abraham continued from fifty down to ten with strong arguments in favor of the land so it would not be destroyed, and God granted his request. Unfortunately, there were not ten righteous people in the whole land. Perhaps, if father Abraham had continued the negotiation until he got God to spare the entire land because of one righteous person, Sodom and Gomorrah would not have been destroyed.

INTRODUCTION TO INTERCESSION

However, he did what every true Intercessor would do. He stood for them, stopped God from continuing his journey to the city, and gave him reasons to abort his plan to destroy the people.

Father Abraham's tactical move, based on his knowledge and experience of who God is and how he works, would have delivered Sodom and Gomorrah from destruction had there been ten righteous people in the land. Genesis 19:29 says God remembered Abraham and sent Lot out of the land when he destroyed it. Although Abraham's intercession couldn't save the whole land, it saved his nephew Lot.

Before I continue, I would like to say that knowing what gives you an advantage from scriptural point of view is very important in prayer. Whenever you read the Bible, try to understand the truth, concept, or principle that the verse, chapter, passage, or story establishes, and use it to analyze every related case you are facing. This enables you to see things from God's point of view and understand his position in every situation.

Biblical truth is the real facts from God's perspective. It is constant, firm, and reliable (it never changes). There are many things the human eyes and mind cannot see or comprehend, and the fact we can't see it does not mean it doesn't exist. The Lord sees what we don't see and he knows what we don't know. When he speaks, he says it the way it really is.

Biblical concepts are notions revealed in the Bible that give us insight to spiritual things. There are key concepts in the Bible that we have to understand, and knowing them gives you confidence.

STRATEGIC PRAYER

The following are few examples: covenant, faith, sin, redemption, justification, salvation, baptism, confession, anointing, etc.

Biblical principles never change. They work everywhere. The principle of sowing and reaping, giving and receiving, birth and death, and day and night are constant. Understanding biblical principles helps you to know how God works. The reason father Abraham addressed God the way he did is because he knew how God works.

Moses was another man who understood intercession strategy, and he used it effectively to defend his people Israel before God while in the desert. Exodus 32:7-14 recounts how the people of Israel corrupted themselves and made a golden calf that they worshiped and made sacrifices to saying, "This is your god, O Israel, that brought you out of the land of Egypt." This made God so angry that he decided to destroy them all at once. Verse 10 says God asked Moses to leave him alone so he could destroy the people and make him — i.e. Moses — into a great nation.

Why would the almighty God ask a mortal man to leave him alone? It appears as if Moses controlled the situation for God to seek his permission, and also made him an offer so that Moses would give him (the Lord) the green light to act. The man held God so firmly that he couldn't do anything among his people without Moses endorsing it. This is what happens when you truly understand intercession strategy. The right use of this game plan puts you in charge of any situation and makes you a commander.

I love how Moses refused the offer to be made into a great nation if he would let God destroy his people.

INTRODUCTION TO INTERCESSION

t highlights the core of intercession, which is selflessness. True intercessors place the interests of others above their own personal desires. No matter how great the offer is, the rules of engagement compel you to make the people your priority. It's all about the people, not self (to defend and protect their interests).

Moses understands how God works and the covenant he made with their ancestors. So he said to God, "Why are you so angry with your people whom you brought from the land of Egypt with a great power and mighty hand? Why should the Egyptians say it was with evil intent you brought them out, to destroy them in the mountain and wipe them from the face of the earth? Turn from your fierce anger, relent and do not bring disaster upon your people. Remember your servant Abraham, Isaac and Jacob, to whom you sworn by your own self to increase their descendant and make the land their inheritance forever." Verse 14 says God changed his mind about the evil he had planned to bring upon his people. He cancelled his plan and gave them another chance because of the intercession of Moses.

Can you just think for a moment about how Moses used the game plan to change the mind of God from wanting to destroy the people to forgiving them their sins? Look at how he tactically changed God's view about the whole thing and engaged his glory and honor by shifting his attention from the sins of his people to what it would cost him if he eventually killed them.

First, he reminded him of what it cost to bring them out of Egypt (a great power and mighty hand),

STRATEGIC PRAYER

Ibefore speaking of what the Egyptians would say at the end of the day (it was with evil intent you brought them out, to destroy them in the mountain and wipe them from the face of the earth). Remember, God told Moses in Exodus 9:16 and in 14:4 that the purpose for which he raised Pharaoh was to gain glory through him, so that his name (the Lord) will be proclaimed in all the earth. Destroying the Israelites in the desert would have aborted that plan and given the Egyptians an occasion to ridicule his great name.

Second, Moses reminded him of how he swore by himself to Abraham, Isaac, and Jacob to increase their descendants and give them the land to inherit. This also engaged God's integrity and steadfastness, because killing them would imply that he was a covenant breaker. Just as everyone would do more to avoid pain than they would do to gain pleasure, God had to change his mind from destroying the people, even though they deserved to die by reason of their sins, because of what it would cost him at the end of the day.

The cost of killing the people was way higher than the honor he would receive for destroying them (the Egyptians would ridicule him, his purpose would be aborted, his oath to the patriarchs would be undermined, his integrity and steadfastness questioned, and he would have been seen as evil and wicked). This would have changed his nature, but God never changes. To prove this, he forgave his people and gave up his plans. The tactics and expertise Moses used to defend his people Israel before God that caused the Lord to spare them from destruction is what I call *Intercession Strategy.*

INTRODUCTION TO INTERCESSION

Moses was a great intercessor who understood the game plan and used it to defend and protect his people from destruction. He was their voice, protector, defender, and advocate. He covered up their sins, weaknesses, and failures, obtained forgiveness from God, and moved him in their favor. One of the important points of intercession strategy is that it gives you advantage and makes you very successful in prayer.

IMPORTANCE OF INTERCESSION

Intercession defends and protects mankind against attack, misfortune, death, and the like. It ensures peace and security amongst humans, and it also brings humanity into alignment and compliance with the will and counsel of God.

Every great move of God on earth is preceded by intercession, and without it, God cannot interfere in human affairs. When God turns his back on humans, the wicked reign and perpetuate evil agendas.

Ezekiel 22:30-31 says God looked for someone among the people to build up the wall and stand in the gap on behalf of the land so he would not have to destroy it, but he found no one. Therefore, he poured out his indignation on them and consumed them with the fire of his wrath by making them pay for their evil works. Intercession secures life and properties.

The reason God seeks intercessors to build up the wall and stand in the gap on behalf of the land so he would not destroy it is that intercession causes him to hold back his wrath. It makes him to bless his people instead of punishing them for their sins.

STRATEGIC PRAYER

God's love for mankind is so deep that he seeks and calls some out to intercede for the others. Hebrews 5:1 says every high priest is chosen from among the people and is appointed to represent them in matters related to God, to offer gifts and sacrifices for their sins. Intercession moves the hand of God and releases his favor.

Job 42:7 recounts how God told Eliphaz the Temanite that his anger burned against him and his two friends because they did not speak well about God as Job did. Verse 8 shows how the Lord commanded them to take seven bulls and seven rams, and go to Job and offer up burnt offering for themselves so Job could pray for them, because God accepted Job, and his prayer would stop the Lord from punishing them for their folly. Verse 9 says that God accepted Job's prayer. Had he not prayed for his friends, God would have punished them.

Job was an intercessor called and approved by God to stand in gap for others. Chapter 1 verse 5 recounts how he sent for his children and had them purified when their feasting period had ended. He would rise early in the morning to sacrifice a burnt offering for every one of them, thinking they may have sinned and cursed God in their heart. This was Job's regular custom, because he was an intercessor called and commissioned to stand between God and the people.

He would break the jaw of the wicked and snatch the prey from their teeth; he would defend the poor, fatherless, helpless and take up the case of strangers. He was a confirmed advocate, mediator, defender, and intercessor of his time.

INTRODUCTION TO INTERCESSION

Whoever heard me spoke well of me, and those who saw me commended me, because I rescued the poor who cried for help, and the fatherless who had none to assist him. The man who was dying blessed me; I made the widow's heart sing. I put on righteousness as my clothing; justice was my robe and my turban. I was eyes to the blind and feet to the lame. I was a father to the needy; I took up the case of the stranger. I broke the fangs of the wicked and snatched the victims from their teeth.
(Job 29:11-17 NIV)

Without someone to stand in gap for the land, things would go wrong. Somebody had to stand in prayer and birth God's agenda for the land and overturn the works of the wicked. This is why God calls someone from among the people to minister unto him in prayer, so he can use their prayer to work his purpose in the life of the people.

Isaiah 59:15-18 declares that truth is lacking, and whoever turns away from evil makes himself a prey. The Lord looked and was displeased that there was no justice. He was amazed that there was no one to intercede. Verses 7 and 18 tell how he put on garment of vengeance to deal with the people according to their evil deeds. Things always fall apart when there is no intercession.

The Lord said through the mouth of the prophet Jeremiah that the reason your injury is incurable, and your wound is beyond healing is because no one pleads your cause. Therefore, you have no remedy.

For thus saith the Lord, "Thy bruise is incurable, and thy wound is grievous. There is none to plead thy cause, that thou mayest be bound up: thou hast no healing medicines."
(Jer. 30:12-13 KJV)

STRATEGIC PRAYER

HOW TO INTERCEDE

Merriam-Webster's Dictionary includes in its definition of the verb "intercede" the following: to try to help settle an argument or disagreement between two or more people or groups, to speak to someone in order to defend or help another person.

The verb *intercede* is a combination of two words; *inter* and *cede*. As earlier mentioned, the prefix "inter-" means between or among, while "cede" means to yield, grant, surrender, give up, relinquish, and so forth. To intercede means to stand between two or more parties and plead the cause of one before the other.

An intercessor is a spiritual defense attorney who takes defensive measures and tactical moves based on his knowledge and understanding of biblical truths, concepts, and principles to protect and defend a person or nation against satanic attack, manipulation, misfortune, or death. He stands on the divine authority Christ gave to the church and uses it to legally defend others in prayer by employing intercession strategy that gives him an advantage, and he uses it in light of God's word to outwit the enemy and rescue the one for whom he prays.

He stands in prayer on behalf of whomever he intercedes for, and uses strategic maneuvers by divine authority to deploy God's hand in favor of the person and break the legal ground of their adversary, in order to silence their voices and overturn their evil works.

First, he diagnoses the situation in light of scripture to understand the root cause of the problem and discerns the basis for demonic aggression before taking a defensive and protective measure in favor of the person,

INTRODUCTION TO INTERCESSION

based on the word of God, in order to render every charge held against the individual baseless through the finished work of Christ on the cross.

Second, he then uses his understanding of scripture to dismiss the case, silence the wicked, overturn their verdict, and stop their onslaught by deploying the blood of Jesus and employing his name according to the written word of God to establish a ground for divine intervention. When God steps in through prayer, he issues a divine injunction that causes the wicked to back off and relinquish their grip on the person. Once the person is free from demonic harassment, everything begins to fall in line.

Based on the structure and order that God established between the heavens and earth in the beginning, the Lord cannot interfere with human affairs unless somebody moves his hand through prayer. Having said that, let's not forget that the hand of God is not moved by all kinds of prayers. It is important we learn how to pray with the right scripture and use the truths, concepts and principles revealed in the Bible to gain the advantage in prayer. This is what makes prayer effective. God does nothing outside his word.

Let me say here that your goal is to use scripture to legally cause heaven to intervene in favor of the person you are praying for, and to then force the wicked to retreat, to give up their grip, and to stop their attack.

To effectively intercede, you must understand scripture, know what gives you advantage, know how to build and present your defense case, understand what gives the wicked advantage, use the blood of Jesus and the word of God to address it, exercise your divine authority and do things in light of the written word of God.

ROLE OF INTERCESSOR

An intercessor is someone called out from among the people by the Lord to stand in the gap before him on behalf of the people and plead their case in prayer. He is very compassionate and he has the people's best interests at heart.

An intercessor is a mediator, defender, negotiator, and advocate who defends and protects the interest of those for whom he stands. He is someone who understands the difference between intercession and warfare, and he is good at taking defensive measures in favor of whomever he represents.

An intercessor is a defense attorney who goes to the courtroom of heaven to defend the cause of other people before the Godhead and the heavenly Sanhedrin. He uses his knowledge, skills, and expertise in prayer to silence the prosecutor (Satan) and render his accusation baseless.

An intercessor is a voice to the voiceless, defense to the vulnerable, and help to the needy. He understands the rules of engagement, the word of God, the wiles of the wicked, intercession strategy, and the ministry of intercession.

An intercessor goes into the courtroom of heaven, accesses the judicial decisions and the executive order of God concerning mankind, and enforces it on earth through prayer. He is an agent of change in the world.

INTRODUCTION TO INTERCESSION

An intercessor is a watchman who stands at the gate, sees into the realm of the spirit, and gives direction to the people as to what they should do. He determines what comes in and goes out of a place (Is. 62:6-7).

An intercessor is someone who understands the ways and acts of God. The Lord does nothing without telling him. He has access to the secret things of God, and the secrets of the people are also made known to him in prayer.

An intercessor not only understands the ministry of intercession but also the art of prayer. He is very passionate about praying for others, and he loves righteousness and stands for the truth. He is a person of integrity who walks his talks.

An intercessor talks less about people's problems and spends most of his time and words in prayer. He does not tell the secrets God reveals to him about someone to another person. And when the Lord opens his eyes to things, he does not share it, unless he is instructed to share the revelation with somebody. He is very discreet and highly discerning.

In summary, an intercessor has a strong desire for prayer, he is passionate about praying for others, and he is always overwhelmed with a burden when he sees or hears about the problems of others. He learns more about prayer and delights in prayer meetings, conferences, or seminars. He is steadfast, truthful, and discreet about spiritual matters. He observes very closely those who are successful in the ministry of prayer and emulates them.

STRATEGIC PRAYER

He always gravitates toward things that add value to prayer. He never speaks against prayer, but encourages others to pray. And he would give up anything to maintain a consistent and effective prayer life. He avoids anything that hinders prayer. He sees prayer as a way of life, learns the rules of conduct, does it with passion, promotes it, and encourages others to do the same.

CHAPTER 2

GUIDES TO SPIRITUAL WARFARE

When the serpent deceived the woman in the Garden of Eden and caused her to transgress the Lord's ordinance by doing what God had instructed she and her husband not to do, the Lord put enmity between the seed of the woman and that of the serpent. He added that the seed of the woman would crush the head of the serpent, while the serpent would strike his heel.

Now the serpent was more crafty than any other beast of the field that the Lord God had made. He said to the woman, "Did God actually say, 'You shall not eat of any tree in the garden'?" And the woman said to the serpent, "We may eat of the fruit of the trees in the garden, but God said, 'You shall not eat of the fruit of the tree that is in the midst of the garden, neither shall you touch it, lest you die.'" But the serpent said to the woman, "You will not surely die. For God knows that when you eat of it your eyes will be opened, and you will be like God, knowing good and evil." So when the woman saw that the tree was good for food, and that it was a delight to the eyes, and that the tree was to be desired to make one wise,

STRATEGIC PRAYER

she took of its fruit and ate, and she also gave some to her husband who was with her, and he ate. Then the eyes of both were opened, and they knew that they were naked. And they sewed fig leaves together and made themselves loincloths. And they heard the sound of the Lord God walking in the garden in the cool of the day, and the man and his wife hid themselves from the presence of the Lord God among the trees of the garden. But the Lord God called to the man and said to him, "Where are you?" And he said, "I heard the sound of you in the garden, and I was afraid, because I was naked, and I hid myself." He said, "Who told you that you were naked? Have you eaten of the tree of which I commanded you not to eat?" The man said, "The woman whom you gave to be with me, she gave me fruit of the tree, and I ate." Then the Lord God said to the woman, "What is this that you have done?" The woman said, "The serpent deceived me, and I ate." The Lord God said to the serpent, "Because you have done this, cursed are you above all livestock and above all beasts of the field; on your belly you shall go, and dust you shall eat all the days of your life. I will put enmity between you and the woman, and between your offspring and her offspring; he shall bruise your head, and you shall bruise his heel."
(Gen.3:1-15ESV)

As I explained under the heading, "Rules of Engagement," the head of the serpent that the seed of the woman would crush symbolizes Satan's authority, government, rulership, and power – that is to say, the authority he took from mankind in the beginning, through deception and manipulation. In revenge, the serpent would strike the heel of the seed of the woman in an attempt to cause him to fall.

GUIDES TO SPIRITUAL WARFARE

The seed of the woman is Christ, and his heel speaks of his body (the church), to whom Christ gave the authority he took from the devil when he offered up himself on the cross as sin offering for the redemption of human souls (Eph. 1:19-23). From the moment Christ defeated Satan and gave the authority he took from him to the church, the devil declared war against the body of Christ. The battle is between the church and Satan, good and evil, light and darkness.

Jesus didn't kill Satan when he defeated him on the cross as some think, he only destroyed his works, stripped him of the authority Adam ceded to him, ended his dominion over mankind, and gave the dominion mandate to the church (Col. 2:14-15, Heb. 2:14-15, 1 Jn .3:8). For this reason, Satan engages the church in fierce battle, contention, and warfare — not to take back the authority Christ gave to us because he can't take it back, but to trouble, shake, and cause instability in the church so that we might lose focus and be distracted from exercising our divine authority.

Whenever Satan strikes the heel of Christ, he shakes his body (the church). This is why some people in the Christendom involuntarily fall in terrible sins or backslide and lose their judicial right to exercise the divine authority (dominion mandate) Christ gave them.

1 Corinthians 10:12-13 warns everyone who thinks he stands to be careful so he doesn't fall. For no temptation in your life is different from what others experience. God is faithful, and he will not allow you to be tempted beyond your ability. When you are tempted, he will show you a way out so that you may be able to endure it.

STRATEGIC PRAYER

James 1:13-16 says that when we are tempted, we shouldn't say God is tempting us, because God cannot be tempted by evil and he never tempts anyone else. But each person is tempted when he is lured and enticed by his own desire. Then, after desire has conceived, it gives birth to sin, and when sin is fully grown, it gives birth to death.

The devil ceaselessly engages our minds and plays with our emotions to make us sin and lose our divine authority. When we sin and remain in it, we fall from grace and forfeit our dominion mandate. But if you confess and forsake your sin, God forgives you and cleanses you by the blood of atonement that Christ shared on the cross for our redemption (1Jn.1:8-10).

The reason Satan keeps engaging the believers in warfare is to make them fall as a way of taking vengeance on them for what Christ did to him on the cross of Calvary. But Christ promised us in Matthew 16:18 that he will build his church and the gates of hell shall not prevail against it. No matter what Satan does, if you can trust God enough and stand your ground in prayer, he will keep the enemy under your feet.

ART OF SPIRITUAL WARFARE

Merriam-Webster's Dictionary defines warfare as activity that is done as part of a struggle between competing groups, companies, and the like. Thus, spiritual warfare is the struggle between good and evil, light and darkness, the church and Satan. This is why the battle we are in is not against flesh and blood but Satan and his cohorts.

GUIDES TO SPIRITUAL WARFARE

Knowing that his time is very short, Satan deployed his army against the church to engage us in continual battle (Rev.12:12).

We are not fighting because we want to; we fight because war has been declared against us by the wicked. Satan, the ruler of this present age, is furious against the church because Christ, the head of the church, destroyed his works, stripped him of his power, shamed him publicly by his victory on the cross, and then gave everything to the church.

2 Corinthians 10:3-5 says that though we live in this world, we do not wage war as the world does. For the weapons with which we fight are not worldly weapons but spiritual ones, which God gave us to pull down strongholds. We silence arguments and every opinion that stands against the knowledge of God, and we take every thought captive to obey Christ, because the wicked engages our minds and plays with our emotions. He uses our feelings, desires, and lusts against us. 1 John 2:16 declares that the only thing the world offers is the lust of the flesh, desires of the eyes, and the pride of life. And since we live in the world, Satan uses what the world offers to trick and trap Christians.

Our thoughts generate feelings, which creates desires, and when desires become very intense, they lead to action. Action produces results, whether positive or negative. If the result is negative, it causes pain, frustration, depression, regret, bitterness, shame, sorrow, tears, and anger. What the devil does is take advantage of these negative emotions and use them to hold people down. Instead of letting them go, he causes them to nurse and hold firmly to them until it becomes a stronghold in their mind.

STRATEGIC PRAYER

Once the stronghold is established, the devil enslaves them by it, and uses it to manipulate them to achieve his wicked agenda.

The art of spiritual warfare is all about repelling demonic aggression, liberating the captives, breaking yokes, securing territories, taking dominion, and defeating the wicked through offensive prayer. It is taking aggressive steps by divine authority to counterattack, withstand, or ward off satanic onslaught.

The art of spiritual warfare is a strategic maneuver that requires a high level of knowledge, skill, and experience, because our opponent the devil, who has been in the fighting business from the beginning, is very sneaky. But we are not ignorant of his devices. We don't fight because we choose to, and the battle has nothing to do with our sins or iniquity — we fight to thwart and overturn every satanic assault, bombardment or offensive. Satan's agenda is to stop, hinder, frustrate, delay, divert, pervert, abort or kill our divine assignment by using any possible means available to him.

The Bible shows us how the Lord Jesus took an offensive and aggressive move to block and silence the devil when he tried to hinder him from fulfilling his purpose (Matt.16:21-23). The passage says that Jesus began to explain to his disciples that it was necessary for him to go to Jerusalem and that he would suffer many horrible things at the hand of the elders, chief priests, and the teachers of the law. He added that he would be killed and on the third day be raised. Peter took him aside and started rebuking him, "Never, Lord! This shall never happen to you." But Jesus turned and said to Peter, "Get behind me, Satan! You are a hindrance to me. You do not have in mind the things of God, but the things of men."

GUIDES TO SPIRITUAL WARFARE

You see here how Satan strategically deployed Peter as an instrument to hinder the fulfillment of Jesus' assignment. Perhaps he did this because of Peter's position or closeness to Jesus. Satan will use whatever he finds as a tool to block the fulfillment of a person's divine purpose. And anything that stands to hinder or block God's will and purpose for your life is a devil that must be stopped. As you engage him by divine authority in this offensive confrontation, you will ward off his aggression and cause him to back off.

Some in the body of Christ don't believe in spiritual warfare. To them, Christ defeated Satan, redeemed us from sins, fought our battles, and gave us authority over the wicked. It is true Christ saved us from sin and death, defeated the devil, and gave us authority over his work, but he did not kill him. The main reason Satan declared war against the church is to get revenge for what the Lord Jesus did to him on the cross.

1 John 3:8 says the purpose Jesus came to the world was to destroy the works of the devil. Christ took from the devil the legal authority to govern the earth that Adam ceded to him in the beginning, and gave it to the church. This is why we are at war.

The Bible encourages us in Ephesians 6:10-13 to be strong in the Lord and in his mighty power and to put on the full armor of God, in order to stand against the schemes of the devil, for we do not wrestle against flesh and blood, but against the rulers, the authorities, the powers of this dark world, and against the spiritual forces of evil in the heavenly places. This is so that we may be able to withstand the enemy in times of trouble, and still stand when it is all said and done.

Whether we accept it or not, we are in a fight, and the target of the devil is to hinder our divine assignment and destroy our destiny. Do not give the wicked any occasion to block your prophetic destiny.

I think this may be one of the reasons the apostle Paul instructed his son Timothy to take his stand, based on the prophetic word spoken about him, and fight a good warfare (1Tim. 1:18). Paul was a good fighter himself, he knew how to hold the wicked off, overturn their evil works and take dominion. The adversary came against him many times in full force to destroy him and stop his assignment, such as when he was beaten with rods, imprisoned, stoned to death, afflicted, threatened, shipwrecked, etc. (Acts 14:19, 2 Co. 11:23-26).

There came a time when more than forty men conspired against him and swore not to eat or drink until they had killed him (Acts 23:12-15). These were different moves orchestrated by the wicked to abort his destiny, but thank God for his grace on Paul's life that enabled him to stand his ground against the satanic offensive. In 2 Timothy 4:7, Paul said, "I have fought the good fight, I have finished the race, I have kept the faith." He fought a real battle as a soldier of Christ and won in order to fulfill his divine purpose.

SPIRITUAL WARFARE STRATEGY

Just like intercession strategy, spiritual warfare strategy is the expertise required for a successful offensive prayer. It is a discipline that must be taught, learned, and practiced by everyone who wishes to master the art of prayer.

GUIDES TO SPIRITUAL WARFARE

The reason many people in the body of Christ suffer defeat or fall in battlefield as they engage the enemy in combat is because they do not understand this strategy.

Spiritual warfare strategy is a game plan based on biblical truths, concepts, and principles. It helps you to discern the wiles of the wicked, focus on the essentials, deploy and employ the appropriate weapons, deter aggression, break yokes, liberate the prisoners, secure territories, take dominion, and conquer the enemies. No army goes to war without a strategy. As soldiers of Christ, you have to know what you are fighting, the main objective for the combat, the tactics to employ when engaging your opponent, and the different weapons at your disposal that you can deploy to defeat your enemies.

One of the reasons many in the body of Christ are defeated by their enemies in battle is that they focus on the wrong things and use the wrong weapons when confronting their opponent. To be successful in this combat, you need a strategy that helps you to understand the schemes of the adversary, how to tackle them, what to focus on, and the kind of weapon to deploy and employ in order to defeat the wicked and block their activities.

When Peter tried to stop Jesus from fulfilling his divine assignment, the Lord looked at him and said, "Get behind me Satan! You are a hindrance to me; you do not have the things of God in mind, but the things of men." Jesus took a strong aggressive move to block this hindrance by addressing the devil rather than Peter, because he knew that Peter was just a vessel that Satan deployed to hinder him.

STRATEGIC PRAYER

Satan was the main source; Peter was the vessel he employed to achieve his aim, while his goal was to hinder Jesus from paying the ultimate price for human souls. The Lord's offensive action was targeted at Satan and his aim. He was the invisible personality hiding in the shadows and using the physical vessel to achieve his aim. Peter was merely the vessel he used for the moment, probably because he was the only one in position to do what Satan wished to do, for no other person among the apostles had the authority to rebuke the Lord Jesus the way Peter did.

The error most people make in the body of Christ is to focus on Peter rather than the source and purpose of the aggression. Peter is simply the means to an end. Satan is the source and his agenda is the end. If you kill the means, he would devise another way to achieve his goal, but when you hit both the source and the end, the means will automatically be grounded. 2Corintians 2:11 affirms that Satan has devices. When one plan fails, he devices another and uses it to attain his goals. Be not ignorant of this fact.

The devil is very cunning; he uses occasion to establish legal grips that give him advantages and judicial rights to afflict, harass, aggress, manipulate, attack, destroy, incite, or frustrate destinies. When you engage him without a proper understanding of the legal right he has by way of an established grip that gives him advantage, you can't defeat him.

To prevail over him, you must first address the legal ground he has already gained, and deal with the devices he's using by deploying the appropriate weapons in prayer. To achieve this, you have to spiritually scan every situation in the light of biblical truths, concepts, and principles to know the kind of spirit at work, their manner and means of operation, their primary aim, why they do it, how to tackle it, what to focus on, the kind of weapon to deploy, when to act, and so forth.

The apostle Paul says in 2 Corinthians 12:7 that because of the abundant revelation he had, a thorn was given him in the flesh, a messenger of Satan to afflict, harass, torment, buffet, or trouble him so that he would not be exalted above measure. So he persistently pleaded with the Lord to take it away from him. But God said, "My grace is sufficient for you, my power is made perfect in weakness." Paul focused on the means (thorn in the flesh) rather than the cause and aim of the whole thing. So he prayed earnestly for God to take the thorn away from him, but the Lord answered him that he could handle it (my grace is all you need, says the Lord).

Let's look at it from a different point of view. Based on the special grace God gave to Paul about Christ and the church, there was high tendency for pride to enter him if nothing was done by the Lord to keep him in check. Paul was caught up to the third heaven whether in body or out of the body, he could not tell, and while in paradise, he heard astounding things that could not be expressed in words — things no human is allowed to discuss. The experience and encounter was so powerful that sharing it with anyone would make people to regard Paul as a superhuman (2 Co.12:2-6).

So great was the apostle Paul that even handkerchiefs and aprons that had touched him were placed on sick people and their sicknesses were cured, and the evil spirits tormenting the people left them (Acts 19:11-12).

STRATEGIC PRAYER

At one point in Lystra, the priest of Zeus and his people almost offered bulls and wreaths to the apostle Paul and Barnabas for healing a man who had been crippled from birth. They called Paul and Barnabas gods in human form (Acts 14:8-13).

The grace the Lord gave Paul to access, apprehend, and comprehend the mysteries of God, from the concept of grace to redemption, adoption, salvation, faith, forgiveness, holiness, rapture, oneness, sacrifice, confession, resurrection, transformation, righteousness, atonement, spiritual gifts and fruit, and governmental authority in the church was so great that some may have possibly thought that Paul was a god in human form.

Since the devil couldn't kill him — though he tried several times — he assigned him a thorn in the flesh, a health condition many Bible scholars and theologians believed was a sickness of some kind that is not proper for a man of Paul's status. For he was often beaten with rods, he received thirty-nine lashes five times, he was shipwrecked three times, and he was once stoned and dragged outside the city to die. Some scholars say the devil orchestrated the whole situation in order to disfigure Paul's face and physical appearance. So he pleaded with the Lord three times to heal him from the illness.

Remember, Paul was a man used by God to accomplish extraordinary miraculous signs and wonders, so that even a simple apron that had touched his body could heal any sickness or disease. For him to suffer such a health condition would cause people to question the authenticity of his anointing and would undermine his authority.

GUIDES TO SPIRITUAL WARFARE

Satan used the condition to torment, afflict, embarrass, and humiliate him, but God used it to keep his servant in check so he did not become proud because of the measure of grace and anointing he gave him for the church.

The Apostle was going through situations and fighting battles that were not the result of his wrongdoing or sins. Many could probably have accused him of some hidden sins for his affliction, trouble, and pain, but scripture informs us that it was due to the greatness of the revelation and grace God gave him for the body of Christ. He pleaded with the Lord to heal him but God kept telling him he could handle it.

Satan used the situation to torment the Apostle and achieve his wicked agenda, but the Lord used it to safeguard his manservant and to keep him from becoming proud. On the other hand, Paul was suffering greatly because of the affliction and pain in his body, even though it humbled him. Sometimes, God allows his servants to go through certain things for a reason.

We have to look beyond the surface by scanning the situation to know the root cause and the primary aim, rather than focusing merely on the means in offensive prayer. Failure to do this may cause the wicked to repel your aggressive actions and make you the victim instead of victor.

A prayer warrior is a strategist, an expert in taking offensive measures against aggression, affliction, manipulation, wickedness, and the like, by engaging the root cause, mode of operation, and the main objective of the thing in order to rescue the victim from destruction.

STRATEGIC PRAYER

Just like David did when a lion or bear took a lamb from his father's flock, he went after the killer and rescued the lamb from its mouth, and when it turned on him, he caught it by the jaw, struck and killed it.

But David said to Saul, "Your servant has been keeping his father's sheep. When a lion or a bear came and carried off a sheep from the flock, I went after it, struck it and rescued the sheep from its mouth. When it turned on me, I seized it by its hair, struck it and killed it. Your servant has killed both the lion and the bear; this uncircumcised Philistine will be like one of them, because he has defied the armies of the living God. The Lord who delivered me from the paw of the lion and the paw of the bear will deliver me from the hand of this Philistine."
(1 Sam.17:34-37 NIV)

Spiritual warfare strategy is a game plan used by all successful prayer warriors to fend off demonic attacks, break yokes, rescue the captives, secure grounds, exercise authority, overthrow the wicked, and frustrate their activities. It gives you advantages because it helps you to carefully evaluate every single situation in the light of scripture before taking action. The Bible admonishes us in the passage below to count the cost before beginning anything so we don't start something we cannot finish.

For which of you, desiring to build a tower, does not first sit down and count the cost, whether he has enough to complete it? Otherwise, when he has laid a foundation and is not able to finish, all who see it begin to mock him, saying, 'This man began to build and was not able to finish." Or what king, going out to encounter another king in war, will not sit down first and deliberate whether he is able with ten thousand to meet him who comes against him with twenty thousand?

GUIDES TO SPIRITUAL WARFARE

And if not, while the other is yet a great way off, he sends a delegation and asks for terms of peace.
(Lk.14:28-32 ESV)

Many engage in a fight they cannot complete or win. In fact, it is not every battle you fight, and the best way to win some battles is to avoid them. When Jesus was born in Bethlehem, King Herod tried to kill him, because wise men came from the east to Jerusalem and spoke about his star. An angel of the Lord appeared to Joseph in a dream and said, "Get up, take the child and his mother, and escape to Egypt, and remain there until I tell you, for Herod is going to search for the child to kill him." So Joseph took the child and his mother by night and left for Egypt, where he stayed until the death of Herod (Matt. 2:13-15).

Why would an angel of the Lord ask Joseph to take the child and his mother and run to Egypt because Herod was going to search for the child to kill him? Couldn't he stand against the army of Herod and strike them down at once? Did God become weak that he could not protect his Son against Herod's attack? God could have instantly destroyed Herod and his army, but he chose not to do so. Instead, he asked Joseph to run to Egypt with his Son and stay there until the death of Herod. This stands to reason that you don't fight every battle, no matter how power you are in prayer. Knowing which battle to engage in is very essential to your success in spiritual warfare.

STRATEGIC PRAYER

LEVELS OF SPIRITUAL WARFARE

There are levels and dimensions of spiritual warfare. The level you are in is determined by what you carry. The enemy doesn't bother about those who are going nowhere in life. The intensity of your spiritual warfare is determined by your level of authority and purpose in life. The higher your level of authority and assignment, the stronger the battle you face. We are not all at the same level, because everyone is unique, and we all have different assignments in life. You may be on the same level with another person, but not in the same dimension.

Judges 14:1-7 describes how Samson went to Timnah and saw there a young Philistine woman that pleased him. He returned home and told his father and mother about his plan to marry the lady. "Get her for me as wife," he said to his parents. His mom and dad answered him, "Is there no acceptable woman among your people, that you should go to the uncircumcised Philistine to get a wife?" But Samson insisted that his parents get her for him. The passage says his father and mother did not know that it was from the Lord, for he was seeking an occasion against the Philistines.

The Jewish customs and traditions forbid that the Israelites marry outside their tribes. The passage says it was the will of God for Samson to marry the lady, but the customs and traditions of his family stood against it and activated the voices of his father and mother against it.

The voices of Samson's father and mother's houses represent the covenant, curses, altars, sacrifices, spirits, words, and so forth, that exists in our houses, which the wicked uses as weapon to fight our prophetic destiny.

GUIDES TO SPIRITUAL WARFARE

Samson had to take his stand against the aggression and resistance of the two voices before he could move to the next level of his life. Had he not succeeded in that, he would not have been able to attain the next level as he walked the path of his prophetic destiny.

Samson went down to Timnah, and at Timnah he saw one of the daughters of the Philistines. Then he came up, and told his father and mother, "I saw one of the daughters of the Philistines at Timnah; now get her for me as my wife." But his father and mother said to him, "Is there not a woman among the daughters of your kinsmen, or among all our people, that you must go to take a wife from the uncircumcised Philistines?" But Samson said to his father, "Get her for me; for she pleases me well." His father and mother did not know that it was from the Lord; for he was seeking an occasion against the Philistines. At that time the Philistines had dominion over Israel. Then Samson went down with his father and mother to Timnah, and he came to the vineyards of Timnah. And behold, a young lion roared against him; and the Spirit of the Lord came mightily upon him, and he tore the lion asunder as one tears a kid; and he had nothing in his hand. But he did not tell his father or his mother what he had done. Then he went down and talked with the woman; and she pleased Samson well.
(RSV)

Having successfully blocked the voices of resistance that would have hindered him, Samson then took his parents to Timnah to meet the lady's parents. As they approached the vineyard of Timnah, a young lion came out of the vineyard and attacked Samson. The Spirit of the Lord came powerfully upon him, and he killed the lion with his bare hands, but he did not tell his father and mother about it.

STRATEGIC PRAYER

No lion attacked Samson the first time he went to Timnah to see the young woman. But the very day he took his parents there to introduce them to the lady's family, so that both families could finalize the plan about his marriage, a lion suddenly came out of the vineyard of Timnah to hinder him. And when the lion came out, it targeted only Samson, leaving his father and mother, who were traveling with him.

The question is, how could three people be on the same journey, and only one is singled out for destruction? The passage clearly states Samson did not tell his parents about it. This means that when he encountered the lion on the way, his parents did not see or know anything about it even though they were all at the same place, doing the same thing, at the same time, going the same direction.

A lion is a killer. It was deployed against him to destroy his destiny because of what he carried. Stopping his father or mother wouldn't hinder the fulfillment of the dream, but killing Samson will kill the vision, so the wicked had to engage him in fierce battle in an attempt to abort his destiny. The battle Samson went through here, which his parents did not experience even though they were all at the same place, is because of what he carried.

As long as the lady remained single in her father's house, the lion did not manifest. But the moment a man came out to marry her, the wicked deployed a lion from her home town to stop the man. Don't forget the young woman was a Timnite and the lion came out of the vineyard of Timnah to kill the man who was coming to marry her.

This stands to reason that the lion was the demonic spirit that controlled the lady's birthplace and family. It waited until Samson approached the lady's home before coming out to kill him.

It seems to me like an invisible line was drawn around her home to restrict her destiny, while the lion was the principality's commission to block every attempt to cross the line. Samson's presence in the young lady's life was going to change everything that concerned her. Therefore, the lion was employed to make sure the woman didn't leave her father's house to fulfill her assignment. They put an invisible line she couldn't cross, and as soon as they saw Samson coming to lift her out of her situation to where she was supposed to be in life, the lion showed up to block everything. Marrying Samson would have made her the first lady of Israel because Samson would rule Israel as judge.

Sometime later, when Samson returned to Timnah for the wedding, he turned aside to see the carcass of the lion he killed when he came to introduce his parents to the lady's family. Now, a swarm of bees had made some honey on the carcass of the lion. He scooped some of the honey with his hand and ate as he went along. When he returned to where his parents were, he gave them some and they too ate it. But he didn't tell them that he had taken it from the lion's carcass.

Samson was born a Nazirite (Jug.13:5), and according to the Law of Moses, he was not supposed to go near dead bodies (Num.6:1-13), for that would defile him. When the lion appeared in its real form, Samson knew it was there to stop him. So, he stood his ground, fought and killed it.

STRATEGIC PRAYER

But when the lion transformed itself into honey, all Samson could see was sweetness, so he scooped some and ate, not knowing that the same honey would later come out of him as a riddle and would destroy his marriage.

The carcass of the lion and the honey disadvantaged him, and he did not know it. This is Satan's schemes and battle strategy. He uses tricks and lies to manipulate people in order to gain advantage over them.

While in Timnah, Samson held a feast, and thirty young men were selected to be with him. All of a sudden, he decided to give the young men that were with him a riddle to solve within the seven days of the feast, and he promised to give them thirty linen garments and thirty sets of clothes if they were able to solve his riddle before the celebration ended. But if they could not solve it, they were to give him thirty linen garments and thirty sets of clothes. "Tell us your riddle," they said.

Samson put forth his riddle and said, "Out of the eater, something to eat; out of the strong, something sweet." When they could not solve the riddle after few days, they called Samson's wife and threatened to burn her and her father's house if she didn't entice her husband to explain the riddle to her. For this reason, she wept before him throughout the seven days that the feast lasted.

On the seventh day, he explained the riddle to her because she continued to disturb him about it. So she told her people the answer to Samson's riddle. *"What is sweeter than honey? What is stronger than a lion?"* Samson got very upset, and left the place, because they used his wife to make him explain the riddle.

GUIDES TO SPIRITUAL WARFARE

At the end of the day, the lady was given to his companion who has been his best man (Jug.14:8-20).

You notice here that when the lion appeared in the beginning, Samson resisted and killed it. But when it turned into honey, Samson scooped and ate it. The honey came out of him as riddle, which later became a lion that scattered his wedding and gave his wife to his companion, *"What is sweeter than honey? What is stronger than a lion*? (That is, from a real "lion" to "honey," then to "Out of the eater, something to eat and out of the strong, something sweet," before turning into "What is sweeter than honey? What is stronger than a lion?")

This was a time-sensitive bomb that exploded when Samson was about to complete the marriage rites and take her home with him. It was a demonic setup to make sure the lady never fulfilled her destiny by giving her to someone in her hometown. In the end, she and her father were burnt to death (Jug.15:6).

That was the beginning of Samson's trouble and battle that eventually led to his death. Had he married the lady, he would not have ended up with Delilah, who caused him to lose his hair, the presence of the Lord, his eyes, and to be bound with chains in jail, making sport for his enemy before he finally died. Both Samson and the lady he married faced all that battle because of what they carried and the assignment they were destined to fulfill in life.

There are many ups and downs in life, and when someone goes through things, others always think the person is suffering the consequences of his sins. But the truth is, people go through things that have nothing to do with their sins.

STRATEGIC PRAYER

Some are too quick to judge without even trying to find out why certain things happen to some people. There could be many reasons behind certain things that happen to people.

It is true that some suffer the consequences of their actions; others suffer the consequences of another person's action. But there are few others who suffer not because of their sins or the sins of another person but because of what they carry. A majority of people are fighting a battle and they don't know how it came about; a combat that is a result of what they carry on the inside (their assignment) rather than what they did wrong. This is one of the reasons some people go through so many battles in life without even knowing why everything seems to be against them.

Some would confess the known and unknown sins in an attempt to get relief, while others would blame everything including God for their situation. And no matter how they try to hide or run, the same thing keeps happening to them. In such cases, the warfare is determined by what they carry, not by what they did wrong. And until they take their stand against the aggression, nothing will ever change.

There are levels of spiritual warfare, but the most aggressive level of all is determined by what you carry on the inside. The Bible describes the kind of warfare Jesus faced from the moment he was born that even made him to run from Bethlehem to Egypt for shelter (Matt.2:1-17). The wicked orchestrated things and used every means possible to hunt him down that he might kill him.

GUIDES TO SPIRITUAL WARFARE

Now after Jesus was born in Bethlehem of Judea in the days of Herod the king, behold, wise men from the east came to Jerusalem, saying, "Where is he who has been born king of the Jews? For we saw his star when it rose and have come to worship him." When Herod the king heard this, he was troubled, and all Jerusalem with him; and assembling all the chief priests and scribes of the people, he inquired of them where the Christ was to be born. They told him, "In Bethlehem of Judea, for so it is written by the prophet: "'And you, O Bethlehem, in the land of Judah, are by no means least among the rulers of Judah; for from you shall come a ruler who will shepherd my people Israel.'" Then Herod summoned the wise men secretly and ascertained from them what time the star had appeared. And he sent them to Bethlehem, saying, "Go and search diligently for the child, and when you have found him, bring me word, that I too may come and worship him." After listening to the king, they went on their way. And behold, the star that they had seen when it rose went before them until it came to rest over the place where the child was. When they saw the star, they rejoiced exceedingly with great joy. And going into the house they saw the child with Mary his mother, and they fell down and worshiped him. Then, opening their treasures, they offered him gifts, gold and frankincense and myrrh. And being warned in a dream not to return to Herod, they departed to their own country by another way. Now when they had departed, behold, an angel of the Lord appeared to Joseph in a dream and said, "Rise, take the child and his mother, and flee to Egypt, and remain there until I tell you, for Herod is about to search for the child, to destroy him." And he rose and took the child and his mother by night and departed to Egypt and remained there until the death of Herod.

STRATEGIC PRAYER

This was to fulfill what the Lord had spoken by the prophet, "Out of Egypt I called my son." Then Herod, when he saw that he had been tricked by the wise men, became furious, and he sent and killed all the male children in Bethlehem and in all that region who were two years old or under, according to the time that he had ascertained from the wise men.
(Matt. 2:1-16 ESV)

God had to deploy an angel from heaven to warn Joseph about Herod's secret plot to search for the child to kill him. What did the baby Jesus do to Herod to make him want to deploy all his army against the child in fierce battle? The answer is that he did nothing against the king. The fight started from the moment Jesus' star appeared. When men came from the east and told him that they had seen Jesus' star, the passage says that King Herod and everyone in Jerusalem were all troubled, so he declared war against him in an attempt to destroy his destiny. The warfare Jesus face is due to what he carried, that is, his assignment.

When you meet the apostle Paul at the moment he was going through hard times due to the activities of the messenger of Satan, who was assigned to afflict him in the body, because of the great revelation he had about Christ (2 Co. 12:7), you might want to judge him or link the affliction to an unconfessed sin. But scripture says the battle he faced was due to what he carried; that is to say, to keep him from becoming proud as a result of the ability God gave him to see into the mysteries of God and unfold the hidden truth about Christ and the church.

GUIDES TO SPIRITUAL WARFARE

We see here that the whole problem the apostle Paul had is because of what he carried on the inside of him, and the purpose he was created to fulfill on earth. This is why more than forty people swore not to eat or drink until they had killed him (Acts 23:12-16). People get caught up in battle for many reasons, but the most aggressive of all is determined by what a person carries that the enemy wants to hinder, kill, or destroy.

Joseph, the son of Jacob, is another man who went through many ups and downs in life, from the pit to Potiphar's house, then to prison, and finally to the palace. The Bible declares that Jacob his father loved him more than any of his other children because he gave birth to him in his old age. So he made for Joseph a coat of many colors. And when his brothers noticed that their father Jacob loved Joseph more than any of them, they hated him and could not speak peacefully to him.

Joseph dreamed about how he was binding sheaves in the filed with his brothers, suddenly his own sheaf stood upright while his brothers' sheaves gathered around and bowed down to his own. When he shared the dream with his brothers, they hated him even more. His brothers said to him, "Do you intend to reign over us? Will you actually rule us?" They hated him the more for his dream and the way he talked about it.

He had another dream and recounted it to his brother, "Listen," he said, "I had another dream: the sun, the moon, and the eleven stars were bowing down to me." When his father heard it, he rebuked him and said, "What kind of dream is that?

STRATEGIC PRAYER

Will your mother and I and your brothers actually come to bow ourselves to the ground before you?" His brothers were jealous of him, but his father kept the matter in mind.

One day, his father sent him to go see how his brothers were doing in the field with the flock, and to bring him a report about their wellbeing. So Joseph went in search for his brothers, and he wandered around in the field until a man found him. The man gave him the right direction to where his brothers were feeding their flock.

As he approached the place, his brothers saw him coming, and they plotted to kill him. "Here comes the dreamer!" They said to each other. "Let's kill him and throw him into one of the pits. Then we will say a wild animal has devoured him, and we shall see what will become of his dreams."

When Joseph arrived where they were, they stripped him of his beautiful coat and threw him into an empty dry pit. When they lifted him up out of the pit, they sold him to the Ishmaelites for twenty pieces of silver and took him to Egypt, where he was sold to an officer of Pharaoh, Potiphar, the captain of the palace guard (Gen. 37:1-36).

The Lord favored him in the house of Potiphar and blessed the works of his hand. When his master saw that the Lord was with him and that he gave him success in whatever he did, he made him overseer of his house and put him in charge of all he had. From the moment Potiphar put Joseph in charge of his household and property, the Lord blessed everything he had for Joseph's sake.

GUIDES TO SPIRITUAL WARFARE

The devil deployed Potiphar's wife against Joseph to seduce him so he could kill his divine purpose, but the man stood his ground against her assault and ran for his life. When she couldn't get him to sleep with her, she filed an accusation against him, which made her husband to put him in jail, the place where the king's prisoners were confined. While in jail, the presence of God was with him, and the Lord gave him favor in the sight of the keeper of the prison (Gen. 39:1-23). From the prison, he went to the palace and became the prime minister of Egypt after he interpreted Pharaoh's dream. King Pharaoh put Joseph in charge of the whole land of Egypt (Gen. 41:1-57).

When you look at the different things Joseph went through in life to fulfill his destiny, beginning from the hatred of his brothers to an empty dry pit, then to the house of Potiphar, where he was seriously aggressed by Potiphar's wife before being placed in prison by his master, and finally to the palace where Pharaoh made him prime minister and put him in charge of the whole land of Egypt, you will agree with me that many people fight battles because of what they carry, not because of what they did wrong. The hatred, pain, affliction, conspiracy, tears, sorrow, struggle, and lack or misfortune Joseph experienced were all because of what he carried (his divine assignment).

There are two main reasons the devil is furiously attacking the church. The first is because of the right to govern the earth that Christ took from him and gave to the church, which then made the church the only entity on earth that has the legal authority to deal with Satan.

The second reason is based on the specific assignment each church is to use the divine authority Christ gave us to accomplish on earth.

Christians are in constant battle with the wicked because of our divine authority, and our assignment in the earth. Thus, the warfare is determined by the divine authority and the assignment Christ gave to us.

ROLE OF A PRAYER WARRIOR

A prayer warrior is a strategist, an expert in taking offensive measures against aggression, affliction, manipulation, wickedness, and so on, by engaging the enemies in order to expose their evil agenda and frustrate their mode of operation.

Prayer warriors are also watchmen who stand on the watchtowers of cities, nations, and regions to ensure safety and security against demonic invasion, harassment, and domination.

They are God's battle-axes and weapons of war. The Lord uses them to destroy demonic kingdoms, break ungodly nations in pieces, overturn demonic horses, chariots, and the charioteer, and to deal with everyone that has yielded himself as a vessel for the wicked to use in perpetuating havoc.

They maintain spiritual peace and stability in a region by resisting demonic aggression and arresting any agents of darkness deployed and commissioned by the wicked to destroy lives and properties.

A prayer warrior uses the different weapons of warfare that God made available to the church to dismantle satanic networks, abort every agenda of the wicked, and overturn demonic activities in the life of God's children.

GUIDES TO SPIRITUAL WARFARE

Prayer warriors are soldiers of Christ equipped by divine authority and commissioned by the Lord to skillfully and intelligently engage the enemies of the church in battle and repel every satanic onslaught against the people of God. They are special vessels that God uses to enforce and superimpose his counsel over the works of the wicked.

Prayer warriors turn the battle to the gates, push the enemy back, overturn their works, secure lost grounds, take dominion, and conquer demonic entities operating in a region. They are aggressive, very sensitive to any sign of demonic presence and operation in a region, and they are always ready to engage the wicked in battle.

IMPORTANCE OF SPIRITUAL WARFARE

Spiritual warfare helps you to take your stand against the schemes and battle strategies of Satan and his cohorts. The devil is very cunning and sneaky. It takes a prayer warrior to abort his evil agenda and frustrate his activities.

Those who master the art of spiritual warfare know how to block demonic aggression, liberate the captives, break all kinds of yokes, secure territories, take dominion and defeat the wicked. Many Christians fall in the battleground and become victims instead of champions because they do not understand spiritual warfare strategy.

As soldiers of Christ, spiritual warfare is not a choice but an obligation. It is our responsibility to defend and protect whatever God has entrusted to our care.

STRATEGIC PRAYER

The Bible declares in John 10:10 that the thief comes only to steal, kill, and destroy. We block every attempt of the wicked to destroy our inheritance through spiritual warfare.

You can break trans-generational curses, destroy demonic arrows, deal with household enemies, bind demonic strong men, resist the devil, change the spiritual climate over a region, and conquer territories through spiritual warfare.

It is one of the ways we exercise our divine authority and dominion mandate. We use it to pull down strongholds, demolish arguments, and overturn everything that sets itself up against the knowledge of God.

The will and counsel of God for humanity is enforced and superimposed over the works of the wicked through spiritual warfare. We all know Satan doesn't play fair. It takes an aggressive prayer to resist him and thwart his wicked agenda.

For you to look at the enemies, and declare war against them, draw the battle line using the blood of Jesus, and order them to stay on their side of the line and not trespass, takes spiritual warfare. It is only through the art of spiritual warfare that you can push the battle to the gate, hold the enemy off, overturn their works, secure the territories, take dominion, and conquer them.

WEAPONS OF SPIRITUAL WARFARE

The Bible declares in 2 Corinthians 10:3-6 that though we live in this world, we do not wage war as the world does, for the weapons we fight with are not the weapons of the world but spiritual, with divine power to pull down strongholds.

GUIDES TO SPIRITUAL WARFARE

You cannot use physical weapons to fight spirit beings. Our adversary the devil and his cohorts are not humans but spirit beings.

Ephesians 6:10 encourages us to be strong in the Lord and in his mighty power. Verse 11 says, "Put on the full armor of God, so that you can take your stand against the devil's schemes." We do not wrestle against human beings but against rulers and authorities, powers of this dark world and spiritual forces in the heavenly places. The devil is very sneaky and scheming. Unless we deploy and employ the right weapons when fighting the wicked, we cannot defeat them.

There are many weapons of warfare Christ gave to the church to fight and defeat the wicked. Prayer, fasting, thanksgiving, sacrificial giving, faith confession, the blood and name of Jesus, testimony, praise and worship, the sword of the spirit, the Lord's Table, prophetic declarations, faith walk, forgiveness, and silence are some of the most reliable weapons of spiritual warfare that Christians can use at any time to engage and conquer their adversaries.

God has equipped us as Christians with different weapons of spiritual warfare that we can use to engage and defeat the wicked in battle. However, we have to learn how to deploy and employ them. Knowing the right weapon to use when facing certain situations is very important. Those who master the art of wielding the sword are experts both in intercession and spiritual warfare.

The word of the Lord Jesus in Matthew 17:21 shows that prayer alone can't do it all. There are things you have to add to prayer to make it more powerful and effective.

STRATEGIC PRAYER

What to add to prayer is determined by the situation you are in, because all conditions are not the same. This is why you have to diagnose every situation spiritually by scanning it in light of biblical truths, concepts, and principles to discern the root cause and determine the appropriate weapon that you need to deploy and employ in dealing with the issue.

Some situations can be dealt with mainly by prayer and fasting. Other stubborn issues need the power of sacrifice, thanksgiving, anointing oil, the Lord's Table, seed faith, prophetic declaration, faith confession, forgiveness, faith walk, rhema word or specific prophetic direction to deal with them.

To be highly effective and successful in prayer, you have to understand the different dynamics involved and master the best prayer techniques that produce results. We use the weapons of spiritual warfare to negate satanic orchestration and block all his activities in our lives and homes.

You have to be sensitive to the Holy Spirit and depend wholly on him when praying for him to direct you as to the kind of weapon to use, whether in spiritual warfare or intercession. Romans 8:26 says that we do not know how to pray, and when we pray, we do not pray as we ought to because of the weakness of our flesh. Depending on the Holy Spirit for inspiration and direction in prayer is very important because he masters the art of prayer perfectly, understands every situation, knows the appropriate weapons for dealing with different issues, and he helps us to do things in accordance with God's will and purpose.

CHAPTER 3

WIELDING THE SWORD

The word of God is the sword of the spirit (Eph.6:17). It is one of the greatest weapons God made available to the church for spiritual warfare and intercession. Hebrews 4:12 declares that the word of God is living and active, sharper than any two-edged sword, cutting between soul and spirit, between joint and marrow; it judges the thoughts and intentions of the heart.

The Lord said in John 6:63b that the word he speaks is spirit and life. The Bible is the revealed written mind and will of God for humanity. Everything must pass the litmus test of the word of God to move the hand of the Lord, because he does nothing outside the truths, concepts, and principles revealed in his word.

Wielding the sword of the spirit is about using scriptures intelligently and strategically as weapons of warfare and intercession. It goes beyond merely quoting scriptures in prayer to your ability to spiritually scan a situation in light of the written word, which enables you to see things from God's perspective before deploying the appropriate weapon to tackle the issue.

STRATEGIC PRAYER

Those who know how to discern things spiritually, interpret scripture correctly, and apply the truths, concepts, and principles of the word wisely gain much ground in prayer and produce positive results. It's not about quoting passages of the Bible, but using it to establish ground and basis that backs up your tactical maneuver in prayer, in order to gain advantage over the adversaries and defeat them.

The Lord Jesus said in Matthew 22:29 that we are in error because we do not know the scriptures or the power of God. The main reasons many struggle in prayer is that they do not understand scripture. Some just open their Bible and read the passage loudly in prayer, while others quote it out of context. Few others hold the Bible in their hands when praying, thinking God will move because they hold his word in their hands.

2 Corinthians 3:6b says the letter kills, but the Spirit gives life. It is the spirit of the word of God that produces life, not the letter. It takes the rhema or the revealed word to move the hand of God in prayer. Rhema is for those who are mature in the things of the spirit, not for babies in the Lord. Hebrews 5:11-15 declares:

There is much more we would like to say about this, but it is difficult to explain, especially since you are spiritually dull and don't seem to listen. You have been believers so long now that you ought to be teaching others. Instead, you need someone to teach you again the basic things about God's word. You are like babies who need milk and cannot eat solid food. For someone who lives on milk is still an infant and doesn't know how to do what is right.

WIELDING TO SWORD

Solid food is for those who are mature, who through training have the skill to recognize the difference between right and wrong.
(Heb.5:11-14 NLT)

Chapter 6:1 of Hebrews encourages us to leave the elementary teachings about Christ and go to maturity. Those who master the art of wielding the sword of the spirit are not babies in the Lord but men and women who can exegetically interpret scriptures and decode biblical truths, concepts, and principles that they use to establish legal ground in prayer. They are expert intercessors and prayer warriors who use the word of God as measuring standard for analyzing things. They interpret every situation in light of the written word of God and do prayer from heavenly perspective.

The Bible declares in Isaiah 43:26, "Review the past for me, let us argue the matter together; state the case for your innocence." God expects us to remind him of the truths, concepts, and principles in his word and use them to establish legal grounds on which we stand in prayer to move his hands and cause him to act in our favor. The legal grounds become the reason for God to move and grant whatever you ask of him. The word of God can be used both as a defensive and offensive weapon in prayer. It all depends on your knowledge and understanding of scripture.

Then Jesus was led up by the Spirit into the wilderness to be tempted by the devil. And he fasted forty days and forty nights, and afterward he was hungry. And the tempter came and said to him, "If you are the Son of God, command these stones to become loaves of bread."

STRATEGIC PRAYER

But he answered, "It is written, 'Man shall not live by bread alone, but by every word that proceeds from the mouth of God.'" Then the devil took him to the holy city, and set him on the pinnacle of the temple, and said to him, "If you are the Son of God, throw yourself down; for it is written, 'He will give his angels charge of you,' and 'On their hands they will bear you up, lest you strike your foot against a stone.'" Jesus said to him, "Again it is written, 'You shall not tempt the Lord your God.'" Again, the devil took him to a very high mountain, and showed him all the kingdoms of the world and the glory of them; and he said to him, "All these I will give you, if you will fall down and worship me." Then Jesus said to him, "Begone, Satan! For it is written, 'You shall worship the Lord your God and him only shall you serve.'" Then the devil left him, and behold, angels came and ministered to him.
(Matt. 4:1-11 RSV)

The passage above reveals how the Lord Jesus used the word of God both to defend himself and repel the devil when he came to tempt him. In fact, Satan used the word as offensive weapon against the Lord Jesus, in an attempt to get hold of him, but the Lord used the same word to counter Satan's aggression.

Having fasted forty days and nights, scripture says that Jesus was hungry. The devil used the need (hunger) in his life as window of opportunity to attack him. He continued, "If you are the Son of God, command these stones to become loaves of bread." Jesus had fasted forty days and night; he was hungry and he needed something to eat.

Mark 1:13 says he was with wild animals in the desert. Wild animals are not found at the backyard but inside the desert.

WIELDING TO SWORD

To stay without food and walk back to the city where he could find something to eat after forty days of fasting and prayer could be very stressful. Satan twisted scriptures and used them as a weapon based on the immediate needs in Jesus' life to make him do things he was not supposed to do. Jesus used the same word to defend himself and block Satan's onslaught.

Another person who understood how to use the spoken word of God in prayer was Moses. As a matter of fact, Moses was one of the greatest intercessor who ever lived in this world. When the people of Israel rebelled against God because of the bad report that ten out of the twelve spies Moses sent to explore the land of Canaan brought to the community about the land God promised to give them, the glory of the Lord appeared at the tent of meeting to all the Israelites.

God said to Moses, "How long will this people despise me? And how long will they not believe in me, in spite of all the signs I have done among them? I will strike them with the pestilence and disinherit them, and I will make of you a nation greater and mightier than they." But Moses refused God's offer and asked him what the Egyptians would say when they heard about it; because God had displayed his power to bring the Israelites out from Egypt with the intention of taking them to the promised land.

"If you destroy them all as one man," says Moses, "the nations who have heard the report that you live among your people, and that you have been seen face to face, that your cloud stays over them, and that you go before them in pillar of cloud by day and a pillar of fire by night,

STRATEGIC PRAYER

will say it is because you were not able to bring them into the land you swore to give them that you have killed them in the wilderness. Please let your power be great, as you have promised, saying, 'The Lord is slow to anger, abounding in love and forgiving sin and rebellion. Yet he does not leave the guilty unpunished; he punishes the children for the sins of the parents to the third and fourth generation.' Therefore, forgive the sin of your people in accordance with your great love, just as you have forgiven them ever since they left Egypt."

When God heard this, he said to Moses, "I have forgiven them as you asked." The man Moses held God by his word and reminded him of what he promised. The Lord had no choice but to act in accordance with his word.

The Lord said to Moses, "How long will these people despise Me? How long will they not trust in Me despite all the signs I have performed among them? I will strike them with a plague and destroy them. Then I will make you into a greater and mightier nation than they are." But Moses replied to the Lord, "The Egyptians will hear about it, for by Your strength You brought up this people from them. They will tell it to the inhabitants of this land. They have heard that You, Lord, are among these people, how You, Lord, are seen face to face, how Your cloud stands over them, and how You go before them in a pillar of cloud by day and in a pillar of fire by night. If You kill this people with a single blow, the nations that have heard of Your fame will declare, 'Since the Lord wasn't able to bring this people into the land He swore to give them, He has slaughtered them in the wilderness.' "So now, may My Lord's power be magnified just as You have spoken:

WIELDING TO SWORD

The Lord is slow to anger and rich in faithful love, forgiving wrongdoing and rebellion. But He will not leave the guilty unpunished, bringing the consequences of the fathers' wrongdoing on the children to the third and fourth generation. Please pardon the wrongdoing of this people in keeping with the greatness of Your faithful love, just as You have forgiven them from Egypt until now." The Lord responded, "I have pardoned them as you requested.
(Num.14:11-21HCSB)

Your level of success in using the sword of the spirit, whether in intercession or in spiritual warfare, is determined by your ability to understand and accurately decode biblical truths, concepts, and principles from the word of God and use them to establish legal ground in prayer. Those who master the act of wielding the sword of the spirit in prayer produce results and do incredible things through prayer. As earlier said, the word of God can be used both as a defensive and offensive weapon. It all depends on your knowledge and understanding of scriptures.

For though we walk in the flesh, we do not war according to the flesh. For the weapons of our warfare are not [a]carnal but mighty in God for pulling down strongholds, casting down arguments and every high thing that exalts itself against the knowledge of God, bringing every thought into captivity to the obedience of Christ, and being ready to punish all disobedience when your obedience is fulfilled.

(2 Co. 10:3-6 NKJV)

CHAPTER 4

BATTLE OF THE MIND

Genesis 6:5 informs us that the Lord saw how great the wickedness of humanity had become on the earth and that every inclination of the thoughts of their hearts was only evil all the time. The human mind is the battlefield for spiritual warfare between the forces of light and darkness. And whatever controls the mind controls the person, because the condition of one's mind determines his words and actions.

Matthew 12:34 says whatever is in the heart determines what comes out of the mouth, and verse 35 declares that a good person produces good things out of the good stored up in him, and an evil person brings forth evil things from the treasury of an evil heart. This could be the reason why the prophet Jeremiah says in chapter 17:9 that the human heart is deceitful above all things and desperately wicked. Who can understand it?

STRATEGIC PRAYER

In Romans 12:2, the great apostle Paul asks us not to conform to the pattern of this world, but to be transformed by the renewing of our mind, that we may be able to discern what is good, perfect, and pleasing to God. The human mind is made up of memory, thought or contemplation, and imagination. These three components deal with past, present, and future events. The memory keeps mental images of past experiences, the thought deals with the now, while the imagination enables you to project into the future and generates mental pictures that play on the screen of your mind.

Our education, experiences, practices, beliefs, perception, and so on, which determine our attitudes are stored in the mind. Both God and Satan engage humans in the mind to gain control over our lives. This is why the mind is the center for spiritual warfare, the struggle that goes on daily within, between truth and falsehood, good and evil, light and darkness. Each party uses strategic plan and weapons to gain control over the human mind, for no spirit can operate legally in this world without a body. And there is no way a spirit can successfully use the human body unless it controls the person's mind.

James 4:4 makes it clear that friendship with the world is enmity with God, for whomever chooses to be a friend of the world makes himself an enemy of God. Satan uses worldly principles, systems, beliefs, customs, traditions, or ways to entice and enslave people to do his will.

Romans 8:7 says the sinful mind is hostile to God because it does not submit to his law and it will never do so. Verse 8 declares that those who are controlled by the flesh cannot please God.

The apostle John writes, "Do not love the world or the things in the world. If anyone loves the world, the love of the Father is not in him. For all that is in the world – the desires of the flesh and the desires of the eyes and pride of life – is not from the Father but is from the world. And the world is passing away along with its desires, but whoever does the will of God abides forever." (1 Jn.2:15-17)

You, however, are controlled not by the sinful nature but by the Spirit, if the Spirit of God lives in you. And if anyone does not have the Spirit of Christ, he does not belong to Christ. But if Christ is in you, your body is dead because of sin, yet your spirit is alive because of righteousness. And if the Spirit of him who raised Jesus from the dead is living in you, he who raised Christ from the dead will also give life to your mortal bodies through his Spirit, who lives in you.
(Rom.8:9-11 NIV)

The scripture above says if anyone does not have the Spirit of Christ, he does not belong to him. I believe the reason is that the Godhead uses the Holy Spirit to infuse his eternal life into the spirit of humans in Christ Jesus, the savior of humanity, for new birth, so the person can be one with Christ in spirit and become member of the universal body of Christ – the church, according to scripture (1Co. 6:17, 12:13). Through the operation of the Holy Spirit, which consists of his ministry, gifts, and fruit, God transforms us into the very image of Christ in words and deeds.

The Holy Spirit uses his ministerial work to perform two works in us. First, to regenerate our spirit from the spiritual death that came on humankind through the sin of Adam the father of human race and make us a new creation in Christ at new birth (2 Co.5:17).

STRATEGIC PRAYER

Second, to renew our mind in light of biblical truths, concepts, and principles (revelation knowledge of the word [Col. 3:10] in order to change our belief system, thought pattern, perception, and words. The ministerial function of the Holy Spirit produces an inward change (spirit and mind) in us and this manifests in words, because words are the expression of thought.

Next, he uses his gifts to change our actions by strengthening our weak zones and reinforcing our areas of excellence for moral activities. He empowers us through his gifts to do things that we wouldn't do on our own, such as fasting, prayer, true love, giving, living for Christ, and so on. This whole process produces a change in our deeds. The last thing he does is to use his fruit to change our character, and this manifested in the way we behave.

In the end, the Holy Spirit produces a new lifestyle in words and actions that reflects the nature of Christ in us through his ministry that changes our spirit and mind (inward transformation), gifts that change our actions (works), and his fruit that changes our character (conduct).

The result that the ministry, gifts, and fruit of the Holy Spirit produce in us is a new way of life in words and actions that reflect Christ (Eph. 4:13). This is why Christianity is not just a religious activity but a standard of living. Have you ever wondered why the Lord Jesus said in John 16:7 that it was to our advantage for him to go away, so that the Holy Spirit will come to be with us and abide with us forever?

I say then, walk by the Spirit and you will not carry out the desire of the flesh. For the flesh desires what is against the Spirit,

BATTLE OF THE MIND

and the Spirit desires what is against the flesh; these are opposed to each other, so that you don't do what you want. But if you are led by the Spirit, you are not under the law.
(Gal. 5:16-18 HCSB)

The repeated struggle, fight, and contention in our mind between the Spirit and the flesh is what I call the *battle of the mind*. On one end is the desires of the Spirit, and on the other end is the desires of the flesh, and the two are opposed to each other so that no one can do both simultaneously. God uses the desires of the Spirit to draw us to himself, while Satan uses the desires of the flesh to draw us to himself. Romans 8:5 says those who live by the dictates of the Spirit set their minds on spiritual things, while those who live according to the desires of the flesh set their minds on things that please and satisfy the flesh.

When the Holy Spirit gets a person's spirit and mind through his ministerial work — which consists of witnessing, reproving, teaching and reminding — he regenerates the person's spirit and begins a renewing work on their mind that is tripartite in nature. That is, memory, thought, and imagination. He starts by deprogramming whatever has been stored in the memory through negative past experiences, practices, customs, beliefs, education, or events, and replacing it with new experiences, values, beliefs, principles, practices, truths, concepts, or events.

He also focuses the person's attention on things that relate to Christ and the kingdom of heaven in order to shape their thought pattern. Lastly, he constantly plays mental images of the envisioned future promised by God on the screen of the person's mind so as to give the person hope and faith about the future, both in this life and the world to come. With this, he produces a new mindset that craves spiritual things in the person. To accomplish this, the Holy Spirit starts a spiritual walk with us by faith and revelation knowledge of the word of God (Eph.4:11-16).

The apostle Paul writes, "If we live in the Spirit, let us also walk in the Spirit." (Gal.5:25) It is one thing to live in the Spirit; another is to walk in the Spirit. To win the battle of the mind and live a successful Christian life, you have to walk the path of faith and righteousness with the Holy Spirit. It takes a spiritual walk to attain to maturity in the things of God, and only mature people can discern and resist deceitful satanic schemes. Those who mainly live in the spirit are babies in spiritual matters; every now and then, they get carried away by the wiles of the devil. I have a lot to say about spiritual life that cannot be fully covered in this book. For more information on this, please go to my book, "The Holy Spirit."

Finally, my brethren, be strong in the Lord and in the power of His might. Put on the whole armor of God, that you may be able to stand against the wiles of the devil. For we do not wrestle against flesh and blood, but against principalities, against powers, against the rulers of the darkness of this age, against spiritual hosts of wickedness in the heavenly places. Therefore take up the whole armor of God, that you may be able to withstand in the evil day, and having done all, to stand. (Eph.6:10-13 NKJV)

For though we live in the world, we do not wage war as the world does. The weapons we fight with are not the weapons of the world. On the contrary, they have divine power to demolish strongholds. We demolish arguments and every pretension that sets itself up against the knowledge of God,

and we take captive every thought to make it obedient to Christ. And we will be ready to punish every act of disobedience, once your obedience is complete.
(2 Co.10:3-6 NIV)

The two passages above inform us that we are in a fight and that the battle is not physical but spiritual. Some unseen forces want to take over our lives and use our bodies as vehicles for achieving their evil agenda, since spirits have no legal authority to operate on earth without body, whether human or animal. For this reason, demonic forces are angrily contending for human bodies to use. And to do that, they engage the human mind in fierce battle day and night using different strategies and techniques to get into our minds and establish strongholds through falsehood, doubt, deception, bitterness, unforgiveness, hatred, frustration, anger, depression, offense, etc.

The easiest way to defeat the enemies and win this battle of the mind is to deploy and employ spiritual weapons that God gave to the church in Christ. I love the way the *New Living Translation* puts it: "We use God's mighty weapons, not worldly weapons, to knock down the strongholds of human reasoning and to destroy false arguments. We destroy every proud obstacle that keeps people from knowing God. We capture their rebellious thoughts and teach them to obey Christ. And after you have become fully obedient, we will punish everyone who remains disobedient." (2 Co.10:3-6)

You may be wondering what these weapons God gave to the church to knock down the strongholds of human reasoning and false arguments really are. The Bible says in John 8:44 that the devil is a liar and is the father of lies.

STRATEGIC PRAYER

Lying is very consistent with the nature and character of the devil because there is no truth in him. One can only give what he has, and since Satan is a liar and the father of lies, he uses falsehood to established strongholds in human mind. Through lies, false arguments, and deceitful reasoning, he sows doubt and confusion that he uses to mislead and ensnare people.

Once he gets the person's attention, he continuous to nurture it with numerous references that strongly support and confirm the idea until it becomes a conviction. He then uses that conviction to create a belief system and thought pattern that shapes the mind in a particular way. Belief creates a sense of certainty in you and causes you to resist, refute, and fight anything that goes against your conviction.

At this level, it becomes a stronghold that the devil uses to hold you down so firmly that nothing else makes sense to you. It makes you very resistant to any opposing ideas, words, or actions, and it will get on your nerves whenever somebody questions your conviction whether by words or deeds.

In the end, it becomes a mindset, the lens through which you perceive, interpret, and appraise the outside world. Whatever happens around you, whether at home, school, place of work, community, or nation that does not agree with your belief about how such things should be done, offends you and makes you bitter, angry, frustrated, depressed, and so on that you would take any action to block or oppose. This is why some people will give an astonishing amount of resources, time, energy, and so forth to a cause others may call an unnecessary investment or a waste of resources.

BATTLE OF THE MIND

The only way to knock down and overturn such strongholds in a person's mind is through the weapon of God's word. Whatever you believe, you don't question. The light of biblical truth exposes the lies of Satan and causes you to doubt and start questioning the lies Satan used to establish the stronghold in your mind.

John 17:17 says sanctify them by the truth, for your word is truth. John 1:17 declares that the law was given through Moses, but grace and truth came through Jesus Christ. John 8:32 makes it clear that when you know the truth, it sets you free. In John 14:6, the Lord Jesus said he is the way, the truth, and the life. No one comes to the Father except through him. The Bible calls the Holy Spirit the Spirit of truth and the Lord Jesus said that he (the Holy Spirit) will guide us into all truth (Jn.16:13).

The prophet Jeremiah says in Jeremiah 23:29 that the word of God is like a hammer that breaks a rock in pieces. Through his ministerial function, the Holy Spirit uses the truth of God's word to refute every deceitful reasoning and false argument that the devil uses to mislead people into error and enslave them. He breaks down every false belief system and thought pattern that Satan used to program the person's mentality and then reprograms the person's mind in light of biblical truths, concepts, and principles from the written word of God in order to create a new mindset in that person.

Behold, the days are coming, declares the Lord, when I will make a new covenant with the house of Israel and the house of Judah, not like the covenant that I made with their fathers on the day when I took them by the hand to bring them out of the land of Egypt, my covenant that they broke, though I was their husband, declares the Lord.

STRATEGIC PRAYER

But this is the covenant that I will make with the house of Israel after those days, declares the Lord: I will put my law within them, and I will write it on their hearts. And I will be their God, and they shall be my people. And no longer shall each one teach his neighbor and each his brother, saying, "Know the Lord," for they shall all know me, from the least of them to the greatest, declares the Lord. For I will forgive their iniquity, and I will remember their sin no more.
(Jer. 31:31-34 ESV)

And the Holy Spirit also bears witness to us; for after saying, "This is the covenant that I will make with them after those days, says the Lord: I will put my laws on their hearts, and write them on their minds," then he adds, "I will remember their sins and their misdeeds no more." Where there is forgiveness of these, there is no longer any offering for sin.
(Heb.10:15-18 RSV)

Therefore, there is now no condemnation for those who are in Christ Jesus, because through Christ Jesus the law of the Spirit of life set me free from the law of sin and death.
(Rom.8:1-2 NIV)

The three passages above show how God planned to put his law in the heart of his people and write it in their mind so that none will need to teach the other person to love the Lord, for everyone will know him from within by the law that will be written in their mind. To accomplish this, the Holy Spirit writes the new law, which scripture calls the *law of the Spirit of life*, in our minds. It is the law that sets us free from sin and death in Christ to live a life of righteousness and holiness.

BATTLE OF THE MIND

1 Corinthians 9:21 calls it the law of Christ, Romans 3:27 calls it the law of faith (it produces the faith that saves us), while James 1:25 and 2:12 call it the law of perfect liberty that sets us free from demonic bondage to live a life of peace, joy, success, and fulfillment on earth.

The next day, as they were on their journey and approaching the city, Peter went up on the housetop about the sixth hour to pray. And he became hungry and wanted something to eat, but while they were preparing it, he fell into a trance and saw the heavens opened and something like a great sheet descending, being let down by its four corners upon the earth. In it were all kinds of animals and reptiles and birds of the air. And there came a voice to him: "Rise, Peter; kill and eat." But Peter said, "By no means, Lord; for I have never eaten anything that is common or unclean." And the voice came to him again a second time, "What God has made clean, do not call common." This happened three times, and the thing was taken up at once to heaven. Now while Peter was inwardly perplexed as to what the vision that he had seen might mean, behold, the men who were sent by Cornelius, having made inquiry for Simon's house, stood at the gate and called out to ask whether Simon who was called Peter was lodging there. And while Peter was pondering the vision, the Spirit said to him, "Behold, three men are looking for you. Rise and go down and accompany them without hesitation, for I have sent them."
(Acts 10:9-20 ESV)

Do you see all God had to do in the above passage to tear down the stronghold in the mind of the apostle Peter that would have hindered him from fulfilling his divine assignment?

STRATEGIC PRAYER

The Lord chose him for the occasion to preach the good news to Cornelius, a Roman military officer, so that he and his family could be saved. But the Jewish customs, practices, and the Law of Moses had programmed Peter's mind to believe that no gentile could be saved.

Peter's belief system and thought pattern disqualified Cornelius, even though God had qualified Cornelius for eternal life. This became a stronghold in Peter's mind that God needed to knock down before the Roman military officer could obtain what God had granted him and his family. Peter had to suffer hunger, fall in trance, and watch a script that God used to demolish the stronghold in his mind and change his perception by telling him that what God has made clean should not be called common or unclean.

The vision caused him to question his values, rules, and beliefs about things that the Jewish customs and the Mosaic Law had firmly established in his mind. As he contemplated the vision and tried to figure out the possible meaning of the trance, the Holy Spirit spoke and dismantled the wall of resistance, hesitation, and opposition that existed in his mind. In verse 28, Peter explained how unlawful and impossible it would have been for him to enter Cornelius home and preach to them to be saved, had God not intervened, broken down the stronghold in his mind, and commanded him to release Cornelius' blessings. This is how serious the battle of the mind is. God had to deploy a strategy to break down the wall of resistant before Peter could embrace the mission and fulfill that assignment.

CHAPTER 5

SPIRITUAL MAPPING

Spiritual mapping is the process of gathering information about a place. It helps you to understand the spiritual climatic condition of the place and the kind of spirit that rules in the region. It involves learning about the different features, activities, special events, important sites, origin, history, beliefs, lifestyle, challenges, names and meanings, some location that have spiritual significance, and so on.

To do this, you ask those who have proper knowledge about the place some important questions that will help you to understand what the people believe in, why they do whatever they do, how they do it, who does it, when and how it started, the kind of spirits operating in the region, and the frequent occurrences among the people. Once the data is collected, it should be analyzed in light of the written word of God.

When the Lord commanded Moses to send out some men to explore the land of Canaan, he sent out twelve men who were leaders in their different tribes with specific instructions to go into the hill country and see what the land was like, and whether the people who dwell in it were strong or weak, few or many. Whether the land in which they dwelt was good or bad, rich or poor, had trees or not, and whether their towns were camps or strongholds. "Do your best to bring me some of the fruit of the land," Moses said to them.

So they went, explored the land, and came back after forty days with some fruit and a report about the land God was giving them. They said to Moses, Aaron, and the whole community of Israel that the land they went to explore flowed with milk and honey but the people who dwelt in the land were strong and their cities were fortified and very large. They added, "We are not able to go up against the people, for they are stronger than we are."

They brought a bad report about the land they had explored, that it devoured those who dwelt in it, and that they were like grasshoppers both in the eyes of the inhabitants of the land and in their own eyes. With these words, they discouraged the whole community of Israel, and caused them to raise a loud cry and weep all night.

At the end of forty days they returned from spying out the land. And they came to Moses and Aaron and to all the congregation of the people of Israel in the wilderness of Paran, at Kadesh. They brought back word to them and to all the congregation, and showed them the fruit of the land. And they told him, "We came to the land to which you sent us. It flows with milk and honey, and this is its fruit. However, the people who dwell in the land are strong, and the cities are fortified and very large.

SPIRITUAL MAPPING

And besides, we saw the descendants of Anak there. The Amalekites dwell in the land of the Negeb. The Hittites, the Jebusites, and the Amorites dwell in the hill country. And the Canaanites dwell by the sea, and along the Jordan. But Caleb quieted the people before Moses and said, "Let us go up at once and occupy it, for we are well able to overcome it." Then the men who had gone up with him said, "We are not able to go up against the people, for they are stronger than we are." So they brought to the people of Israel a bad report of the land that they had spied out, saying, "The land, through which we have gone to spy it out, is a land that devours its inhabitants, and all the people that we saw in it are of great height. And there we saw the Nephilim (the sons of Anak, who come from the Nephilim), and we seemed to ourselves like grasshoppers, and so we seemed to them."
(Num. 13:25-33 ESV)

      The members of the community of Israel were crying and grumbling against Moses and Aaron because of the bad report they heard concerning the land God promised to give them. They said, "If only we had died in Egypt! Or in this wilderness! Why is the Lord bringing us to this land only to fall by the sword? Our wives and children will be taken as plunder. Wouldn't it be better for us to go back to Egypt?" This made Moses and Aaron fall on their faces before the whole community of Israel.

      Then Joshua, the son of Nun, and Caleb, the son of Jephunneh, who were among the twelve men sent to explore the land, tore their clothes and said to the whole congregation, "The land we passed through and explored is exceedingly good. If the Lord is pleased with us, he will lead us into that land, a land flowing with milk and honey, and will give it to us.

STRATEGIC PRAYER

Only do not rebel against the Lord. And do not be afraid of the people of the land, because we will devour them. Their protection is gone, but the Lord is with us. Do not be afraid of them."

The twelve saw the same thing and had the same experiences in the expedition, but Joshua and Caleb interpreted things differently. The Bible says they had a different spirit from the other ten (Num.14:1-24). In spiritual mapping, we must see things from a different perspective and interpret them in light of biblical truths, concepts, and principles.

When Joshua succeeded his master as leader of Israelite community, he secretly sent out two men to go spy out the land. He said to them, "Go, look over the land, especially Jericho." So they went and entered the house of a prostitute named Rehab and stayed there. The lady took them up to the roof of her house and hid them under the stalks of flax she had laid out. Those who had noticed their presence told the king of Jericho that some Israelites came to the land to spy it out.

So the king sent this message to Rahab the prostitute: "Bring out the men who have come to you, who entered your house, for they have come to search out all the land." But she lied to the king's messengers and said, "Yes, the men came to me, but I did not know where they had come from. And when the gate was about to be closed at dark, they went out. I don't know where they went. Go after them quickly; you may catch up with them." The king's men went looking for the spies Joshua had sent to spy out the land, and the city gate was shut as soon as the pursuers had gone out, to stop the spies from escaping.

SPIRITUAL MAPPING

This is why precaution must be taken when doing spiritual mapping. The wicked know what you carry, the mission and mandate Christ gave to you. So they will do anything to resist or harm you if they uncover your mission. Had God not used Rahab to help the two spies, they would have died, because the enemy came seeking to kill them.

Then Joshua son of Nun secretly sent two spies from Shittim. "Go, look over the land," he said, "especially Jericho." So they went and entered the house of a prostitute named Rahab and stayed there. The king of Jericho was told, "Look! Some of the Israelites have come here tonight to spy out the land." So the king of Jericho sent this message to Rahab: "Bring out the men who came to you and entered your house, because they have come to spy out the whole land." But the woman had taken the two men and hidden them. She said, "Yes, the men came to me, but I did not know where they had come from. At dusk, when it was time to close the city gate, the men left. I don't know which way they went. Go after them quickly. You may catch up with them." (But she had taken them up to the roof and hidden them under the stalks of flax she had laid out on the roof.) So the men set out in pursuit of the spies on the road that leads to the fords of the Jordan, and as soon as the pursuers had gone out, the gate was shut.
(Josh.2:1-7 NIV)

Before Nehemiah came to build the broken wall of Jerusalem, he first inquired about the Jewish remnant who survived the exile and also about the state of the city of Jerusalem from Hanani, one of his brothers, and some other men who came from Judah with him. They told him things weren't going well with those who returned to the province of Judah.

STRATEGIC PRAYER

"They are in great trouble and disgrace. The wall of Jerusalem is broken down, and its gates have been burned with fire."

When Nehemiah heard these things, he wept, mourned, fasted, and prayed to God. From what he heard about Jerusalem, the burden to rebuild the broken wall came heavily on him. Having obtained favor and permission from the King Artaxerxes to rebuild the ruined city of Judah, he went to Jerusalem with army officers, horsemen, and the king's letters to the governor of the province beyond the river.

When he got to Jerusalem, he stayed there for about three days before going out with few others by night to inspect the wall of Jerusalem that was broken down and the gate that had been destroyed by fire. None of the officials knew what he was doing, because he did not tell anyone what God had put in his mind to do for Jerusalem. He went about gathering information regarding the place, the kind of work to be done, what was required to change things, and then planned accordingly before taking action. As soon as they started the work, Sanballat the Horonite, Tobiah, and Geshem the Arab heard about it, and they reacted and did all them could to stop the work.

In spiritual mapping, wisdom and discretion is highly required. There are demonic spirits called strongmen guiding every region or territory who ensure the safety and security of the area. They will react aggressively to any attempt to liberate the region from their grips. When spying out the land, you have to be very careful. The purpose of spiritual mapping is to gather information about a place, plan, attack, liberate, and conquer the region.

CHAPTER 6

SATAN'S SCHEMES AND BATTLE STRATEGY

Satan uses occasion to establish legal ground on which he stands to carry out his evil agenda. Since spirits can't operate legally on earth without a human body, he uses the occasion to establish grips on people's lives and assign them spirit entities to work through them as a means or vessel to achieve his wicked aims.

To have an occasion against a person, he uses any of the following: sin, lies, deception, manipulation, bitterness, anger, hatred, depression, delay, sorrow, frustration, disobedience, disloyalty, rebellion, immorality, addiction, doubt, abuse, rejection, violence, shame, weakness, humiliation, pride, pain, curses, affliction, discouragement, and the like.

When any of the above negative emotions is firmly established in a person, he then uses it as a tool to control the individual at will by assigning him a demonic spirit with an agenda. The evil spirit begins to use the person as a vehicle to achieve his goals.

STRATEGIC PRAYER

The nature of spirit assigned to the person and the agenda Satan uses him to achieve depends on who the individual is, the position he occupies, and the role he plays.

A closer look at the story of Jesus and Peter reveals how Satan can manipulate people and turn them against each other to achieve his wicked agenda. The Lord Jesus started explaining to his disciples in the passage that it was necessary for him to go to Jerusalem and suffer many things at the hands of the elders. He also told them how he would be killed, but on the third day, he would be raised.

When Peter heard this, he took him aside and started rebuking him in an attempt to stop him (Jesus) from going to the cross and save humanity from sin and death. Peter didn't realize he was standing on the path of Jesus divine purpose and prophetic destiny. But when Jesus looked at Peter, he noticed Satan had taken hold of him to use as a vessel to hinder him from fulfilling his divine purpose. So he looked beyond Peter and uncovered the devil that was trying to use him, and he intercepted his strategy and blocked his aggression.

He said, "Get behind me, Satan!" not "Get behind me, Peter," because the man was just a vessel Satan employed for the occasion. And killing Peter wouldn't bring a lasting solution, but identifying the devil behind the scene, uncovering his strategy, and stopping his aggression would produce a permanent solution to the problem.

Our major problem is that we focus on the vessel instead of the one using it against us — that is, Satan's schemes

SATAN'S SCHEMES AND BATTLE STRATEGY

and battle strategy that he uses in distracting people in order to keep them in perpetual bondage.

The story in 1 Kings 21:1-16 shows how Satan works to destroy lives and abort people's destinies. The story is about a man named Naboth, from Jezreel, who owned a vineyard that his ancestors passed to him. The vineyard was beside the palace of King Ahab in Samaria.

The king asked Naboth to give him the vineyard so that he may use it for a vegetable garden, since it was close to his palace. He promised to give him another vineyard in exchange or pay whatever it is worth in money. But Naboth replied, "The Lord forbids that I should give you the inheritance of my fathers." This made Ahab angry and sullen that he went home, turned his face to the wall in bed, and refused to eat.

When his wife Jezebel asked him why he didn't eat, he told her it was because of Naboth the Jezreelite, whom he asked to sell him his vineyard or take another one in its place, but refused and said, "I will not give you my vineyard."

Jezebel said to him, "Is this how you act as king over Israel? Get up and eat! Cheer up. I'll get you the vineyard of Naboth the Jezreelite." Then she wrote letters in Ahab's name, sealed them with his seal, and sent them to the elders and other leaders who lived in the town where Naboth lived.

In the letters, she instructed them to gather the people for fasting and prayer and seat Naboth in a prominent place among the people, and then seat two worthless men opposite him who will accuse him of cursing God and the king.

STRATEGIC PRAYER

Once this was done, they were to take him outside and stone him to death.

When the leaders living the same city with Naboth got the letters, they followed the instruction Jezebel gave and did all she commanded them to do. They proclaimed a fast, sat Naboth in a place of honor, and got two scoundrels men to lay charges against him before the people that Naboth cursed God and the king. So they took him outside the city and stoned him to death.

As soon as Naboth died, they sent word to Jezebel that he had been stoned to death. Then she said to Ahab the king, "Arise, take possession of the vineyard of Naboth the Jezreelite, which he refused to give you for money, for Naboth is not alive, but dead."

You notice in the passage that when the king came directly to Naboth and requested his vineyard, which his father gave to him, Naboth resisted the move and defended his inheritance. But when Jezebel changed the strategy and employed a new technique by offering him promotion, glory, and honor among his people, he could not discern that the prominent seat given to him by the leaders of his community was death in disguise — a scheme carefully devised by Jezebel to kill him and take his inheritance that he had been protecting from the king.

Until Jezebel sent the leaders of his town the letters, they had no hidden agenda against Naboth. The letter was the tool Jezebel used to influence and turn the leaders in Naboth's community against their own brother and kill him.

No one could ever imagine that Jezebel had hand in the death of Naboth, because she worked and controlled things from behind the scenes.

SATAN'S SCHEMES AND BATTLE STRATEGY

She was the master planner and the brain behind Naboth's death, even though she wasn't there in person to execute it.

2 Timothy 2:26 talks about those whom the devil has taken captive to do his will, while Ephesians 2:2 says there is a spirit that is at work in those who refuse to obey God. This spirit is the prince or commander of the power of the unseen world. It uses the patterns, systems, ways, and principles of the world to ensnare and enslave people to fulfill his wicked agenda.

Satan is a very cunning and sneaky strategist who plays on people's ignorance, negligence, and weakness to destroy their lives or keep them in perpetual bondage. He observes their attitudes, mindset, and belief systems, and takes advantage of the loopholes in their lives to either enslave or destroy them. The apostle Paul says that Satan might not outwit us, for we are not ignorant of his schemes (2 Co.2:11). He said that because he knows Satan is very scheming and well-organized.

There is a story in Matthew 12:43-45 that shows how organized the kingdom of Satan is. The passage says that when an unclean spirit leaves a person, it goes out through dry places seeking rest, and if it does not find any, it will return to the house it left. When it arrives, it finds it unoccupied, swept, and put in order. It goes and takes with it seven other spirits more wicked and powerful than itself, and they will all enter the person and live there. It says the final condition of that person will be worse than the first.

The spirit knows that if it goes back to the person and lives there alone, what defeated it before and drove it out of the body could come back and do it again.

STRATEGIC PRAYER

It wasn't scared or insecure to invite other stronger and more powerful spirits than itself to live in the person. Demons know how to staff their weakness and work in unity.

It is written, "For we are not fighting against flesh-and-blood enemies, but against evil rulers and authorities of the unseen world, against mighty powers in this dark world, and against evil spirits in the heavenly places" (Eph. 6:12 NLT). All these spirits work together to fulfill the agenda of their master, Satan, the archenemy of the church.

There is another example in Mark 5:1-15 that throws more light on this point. When the Lord Jesus arrived in the region of Gerasenes, a man possessed by an evil spirit came out from the tomb to meet him. The passage says he lived in the cemetery and no one could bind him anymore, not even with chains, because he had often been bound hand and foot with chains and shackles, but he tore the chains apart and broke the shackles in pieces. He was always crying out and cutting himself with stones as he wandered day and night among the tombs and on the mountains.

When he saw Jesus from a distance, he ran and fell on his knees in front of him, and shouted at the top of his voice, "What have you to do with me, Jesus, Son of the Most High God? I adjure you by God, do not torment me." The following verse says Jesus had already commanded the spirit to come out of the man.

I believe the Lord noticed something was wrong that he decided to ask him what his name was. And the spirit replied, "My name is Legion, for we are many." Then the evil spirits begged him earnestly not to send them out of the area. "Send us into those pigs," the spirits begged Jesus.

SATAN'S SCHEMES AND BATTLE STRATEGY

At first, the spirit presented itself as one, "What have you come to do with me," the spirit asked, and the Lord addressed it as one person and commanded it to go out of the man. This is deception in the highest order. But the Lord noticed something was wrong, so he asked about its name and uncovered its true identity.

A legion is believed by many theologians and Bible scholars to be about six thousand spirits. As soon as the Lord uncovered its identity, the spirit changed from me to us. The spirits were actually saying to the Lord that they are one in purpose, words, and work. Together they stand or fall. When the lead spirit spoke, they all gave it their support and refused to let it fall alone. It enjoyed the support and strength of over six thousand demons as it spoke to the Lord. And when Jesus instructed it to go out, they all stood together and spoke one word: "Send us into those pigs."

Another character in the Bible whose life and work portrays Satan's schemes and battle strategy in many ways is Pharaoh, the king of Egypt. The Bible declares that when he came to power, he devised a plan to hinder the Israelites from increasing in the land of Egypt for fear that they could turn against him, join his enemy in war, and leave Egypt.

So he afflicted, oppressed, and made the lives of the Israelites bitter with hard labor and all kinds of work in the field, and he did not regard any of the things Joseph did to save Egypt when the whole world suffered a season of famine that lasted seven years.

He called the Hebrew midwives, whose names were Shiphrah and Puah, and said to them, "When you help the Hebrew women in childbirth and observe them on the delivery stool, if it is a boy, kill him; but if it is a girl, let her live."

STRATEGIC PRAYER

Remember, the Israelites had been made to build Pithom and Rameses as store cities for Pharaoh and to do all manner of work in the field for the Egyptians. Logic demanded he keep the men alive to have more workforces for his project. But since he knew through divination that one of the Hebrew women would give birth to a deliverer, who would liberate the people of Israel from bondage, he deployed their midwives against them to kill their male babies as soon as they were born.

Midwives are special agents trained to assist women in childbirth. They know everything about the condition, strength, and weakness of a pregnant woman, and women confide in them and tell them their secrets, fears, and concerns. This was the instrument Pharaoh decided to deploy against the women who carried the prophetic seed in their womb. He also instructed them to wait until the women were in the labor ward getting ready to give birth — a strategic moment when the testimony, glory, fruit, blessing, and promotion was about to manifest. That is how Satan works.

The devil is very cunning and well-organized, and he uses spirits and things to deceive and bring people into bondage so he could manipulate them and destroy their destinies. He uses the lust of the flesh, lust of the eyes, and the pride of life to deceive humans, enslave them, and cause them to trade their purpose and destiny for money, fame, and pleasure. To achieve this, he devises ways to make things that are morally unacceptable look harmless to the society in order to create a societal norm that encourages such practices, and in the end, he uses pride, shame, drugs, sex, jail, suicide, and the rest to destroy them.

CHAPTER 7

BREAKING DEMONIC ALTARS

An altar is a place of sacrifice, covenant, fellowship, and worship. It is where divinity meets humanity, the borderline between the world of the spirit and human world. An altar is the only gateway to the invisible world. It carries the name and attracts the presence of the very deity it is dedicated to.

Whatever men offer deliberately to a spirit is always done on the altar that represents the spirit to whom it is offered. It attracts the presence of the very deity it represents, and gives you clear insight and foresight to the nature of the deity it represents, because an altar is the face and eyes of the spirit it represents.

It is the only platform that bridges, connects, and holds two separate worlds together — that is, the spirit and human world. No human can access the world of the spirit without an altar, and no spirit can relate to humans without an altar. Whenever humans go to the altar, they seek audience with the spirit that the altar represents, and any sacrifice offered on such altar goes to that spirit.

STRATEGIC PRAYER

In fact, every altar requires a sacrifice to be activated, and it is the sacrifice on an altar that causes it to speak.

An altar of earth you shall make for me and sacrifice on it your burnt offerings and your peace offerings, your sheep and your oxen; in every place where I cause my name to be remembered I will come to you and bless you. And if you make me an altar of stone, you shall not build it of hewn stones; for if you wield your tool upon it you profane it. And you shall not go up by steps to my altar, that your nakedness be not exposed on it.
(Ex.20:24-26 RSV)

We notice in the above scripture that an altar is a designated place where sacrifices are offered to God. It is also a place that God comes to bless his people. There were rules as to how the altar was to be made, the types of sacrifices to be offered on it, and the manner people went up to it in order not to defile or desecrate it. God receives whatever is sacrificed on the altar and blesses his people.

Genesis 8:20-22 recounts how Noah built an altar to the Lord when he, his family, and all that were in the ark with him came out. He took some of the clean animals and sacrificed them on the altar to God. The passage says when God smelled the pleasing aroma, he said in his heart, "I will never again curse the ground because of man, even though the intention of human heart is evil from childhood. Neither will I again destroy every living creature as I have done. As long as the earth remains, seed times and harvest, cold and heat, summer and winter, day and night will never cease." What follows is that God blessed Noah and his children (Gen.9:1-2).

BREAKING DEMONIC ALTARS

We notice how Noah's sacrifice attracted God's presence and voice. As soon as Noah built the altar, he offered sacrifices on it to the Lord. The offering went up to God as sweet aroma and caused him to speak and act in favor of the one that made the sacrifice. Without the sacrifice, the altar has no power. The spirit does not seek altars but the sacrifices that are offered on them, and when men stop sacrificing on the altar or offer the wrong sacrifice on the altar, the deity to whom it was raised will withdraw from the place.

Leviticus 17:11 says the life of a being is in the blood, and it is only blood that can make atonement for one's life. When sacrifices are offered on the altar, it is killed to bring out the real life that is in the blood. As the blood flows on the altar, the life of the animal is taken through the blood we shed on the altar.

Genesis 4:10 declares that the blood of Abel cried out to the Lord from the ground. Genesis 4:11 shows how the ground that opened its mouth to receive Abel's blood from the hand of Cain rose and worked against him (Cain), because the voice of Abel was speaking through the blood that entered the ground.

Likewise, when a sacrifice is offered on an altar, the spirit it represents receives the life of the animal through the blood on the altar, which then gives voice to the altar. Just as Abel's blood spoke from the ground and attracted the voice of God in judgment against his brother Cain, the blood on the altar gives it a voice and attracts the voice of the spirit it represents against whoever the sacrifice was made.

For better understanding, the sacrifices offered on any altar give voice to the altar, while the voice of the altar amplifies the voice of the spirit it represents.

STRATEGIC PRAYER

A sacrifice is something of great value that pleases whomever it is given to. Every sacrifice has value, and it is the value of a sacrifice that determines its impact; the greater the value, the greater its impact.

Since an altar links, connects, bridges, and holds humans and spirits together, it gives the spirit the legal right to operate on earth. The world is man's domain, and only humans have the judicial rights to operate in it. When we raise an altar to any spirit and offer sacrifices on it, we give the spirit behind it the lawful right to operate in that very region or domain.

An altar amplifies the voice of spirit being and gives them lawful right to operate in the world, while sacrifices activate an altar and give it a voice. Spirit beings receive from humans whatever we offer them on the altar and uses it to work for mankind. Every transaction or trade between the spirit world and humans always happens on the altar.

Demonic altars are those raised to evil spirits by men that give them the lawful right to act on earth. It could be in the family, community, region, state, or nation. The sacrifices made on such altars amplify the voices of the demons in the place and give them legal rights to carry out their evil agenda in that territory (Lev. 17:7, Deut. 32:17, Ps. 106:37).

Without sacrifices, the altar has no power, and without the altar that establishes platforms, bridges, and connections between the human and the spirit world, spirits would have no rights to operate in this world.

BREAKING DEMONIC ALTARS

When dealing with demonic altars, there are few things to target. The first is the human being that made the agreement and establishes the platform. The second is the spirit that is represented by the altar. The third is the altar that bridges or connects the two parties. The fourth is the sacrifices offered on the altar. The fifth is the agreement or covenant established by the altar and sacrifices. The sixth is the effects or consequences of the agreement made between the two parties. The seventh is that you have to raise another altar to thwart the power and grip of the old one that was destroyed.

Be careful not to make a treaty with those who live in the land where you are going, or they will be a snare among you. Break down their altars, smash their sacred stones and cut down their Asherah poles. Do not worship any other god, for the Lord, whose name is Jealous, is a jealous God. Be careful not to make a treaty with those who live in the land; for when they prostitute themselves to their gods and sacrifice to them, they will invite you and you will eat their sacrifices. And when you choose some of their daughters as wives for your sons and those daughters prostitute themselves to their gods, they will lead your sons to do the same.
(Ex.34:12-16 NIV)

You shall surely destroy all the places where the nations whom you shall dispossess served their gods, on the high mountains and on the hills and under every green tree. You shall tear down their altars and dash in pieces their pillars and burn their Asherim with fire. You shall chop down the carved images of their gods and destroy their name out of that place. You shall not worship the Lord your God in that way.

STRATEGIC PRAYER

But you shall seek the place that the Lord your God will choose out of all your tribes to put his name and make his habitation there. There you shall go, and there you shall bring your burnt offerings and your sacrifices, your tithes and the contribution that you present, your vow offerings, your freewill offerings, and the firstborn of your herd and of your flock. And there you shall eat before the Lord your God, and you shall rejoice, you and your households, in all that you undertake, in which the Lord your God has blessed you.
(Deut.12:2-7 ESV)

When the angel of the Lord appeared to Gideon, who was threshing wheat in a winepress to hide it from the Midianites, he said, "The Lord is with you, O mighty man of valor." Gideon said to him, "If the Lord is with us, why has all this happened to us? Where are all his wonders that our fathers told us about? Didn't they say, 'Did not the Lord bring us up out of Egypt?' But now the Lord has abandoned us and given us into the hand of Midian." The angel turned to him and said, "Go in this might of yours and save Israel from the hand of Midian…"

I believe the strength of Gideon was his revelation knowledge about the nature of the God of Israel. He knew the reason Israel was oppressed by their enemies was because the Lord had abandoned them and handed them over to their enemies. He believed it was impossible for God to be with them and their enemies to rule over them. To him, the presence of God worked wonders and brought victory to his people.

Instead of focusing on his knowledge of who God really was and what he was capable of doing when he was with a man,

BREAKING DEMONIC ALTARS

Gideon turned and focused on the condition of his family and his own position in his father's house. The angel spoke again and said to him, "I will be with you, and you shall strike down the Midianites as one man." This was Gideon's strength, the understanding and belief he had about the power and presence of God. He knew for sure that when God was involved, things would turn out well.

The passage points out how the angel instructed him that same night to tear down the altar his father made to Baal and to also cut down the Asherah pole beside it. In addition, the angel asked him to build an altar to the Lord God using the wood of the Asherah pole that he cut down, and the second bull as a burnt offering on the altar. The altar of his father's house and the sacrifices offered on it had limited him; to break out, he would first have to tear the altar down to liberate his destiny from its grip and then raise another altar that would speak in his favor and propel him to his divine purpose.

It takes an offensive prayer to break demonic altars because you engage the spirit in spiritual warfare to overturn their mandate, break their holds, silence their voice, liberate the captives, break the covenant, nullify the sacrifice, liberate the human vessel from their camp, block the consequences of their actions, bind the strongman or cast the spirit out, secure the territory, repel aggression, shift the spiritual climate, block all the channel or means use by the demons to achieve their wicked agenda, and so on using the necessary weapons in prayer.

STRATEGIC PRAYER

What follows is that you raise a new altar by the superior blood of the Lord Jesus, being the ultimate sacrifice offered on earth in favor of humanity that gives the Godhead and the Holy Spirit the judicial right to acts on earth. To be successful in this operation, you have to understand intercession strategy, weapons of spiritual warfare, spiritual mapping, Satan's schemes and battle strategy, wielding the sword, etc.

CHAPTER 8

BREAKING TRANSGENERATIONAL CURSES

According to my papa, the Archbishop Duncan-Williams, "Trans-generational curses simply have to do with patterns of the bloodline." To him, there are things imbedded in our DNA, in our sub-consciousness, and in our bloodline that was programmed by the enemy to restrict and to limit how far we go in life.

Merriam-Webster's Dictionary defines the word curse as "magical words that are said to cause trouble or bad luck for someone or the condition that results when such words are said."

Trans-generational curses are words or actions that have ability to harm, destroy, or cause bad luck spoken over somebody or done by a person for some reason that cause evil to happen to the person and the generation after him. It could also mean a situation that occurs as the result of such words or actions. The misfortune resulting from such words or actions travel through the person's bloodline from one generation to another.

STRATEGIC PRAYER

And if nothing is done to stop the consequences of such words or actions, it will continue to travel in that lineage until it creates a specific pattern in the bloodline that affects the people in such family.

The Lord declares in Exodus 20:5 that he is a jealous God who punishes the children of those who hate him for the sins of their parents to the third and fourth generation. We notice in this verse that the consequences of some actions can travel three or four generations down the line.

God says he punishes the children of those who hate him for the actions of their parents until the fourth generation if the pattern is not interrupted. There is a *cause* and *effect* relationship between the punishment imposed by God on the children of those who hate him and the sins of their fathers until the fourth generation. To stop such punishment that causes a pattern in the bloodline, which affects four generations, you have to address the root cause in order to uncover the sin or action that provoked the punishment.

Using the cause and effect approach or the root cause analysis method in light of the written word of God, you can uncover the origin of certain occurrences in your family, know why they happen, and how to stop them.

Things happen to many people that are not the result of their wrongdoing, but the consequences of what somebody at one point in time did in their lineage. Scripture reveals how Joshua put a curse on anyone who tried to rebuild the city of Jericho after the wall collapsed when the children of Israel gave a loud shout at the sound of the trumpet,

BREAKING TRANSGENERATIONAL CURSES

"Far be it from me; for those who honor me I will honor, and those who despise me shall be lightly esteemed. Behold, the days are coming, when I will cut off your strength and the strength of your father's house, so that there will not be an old man in your house. Then in distress you will look with envious eye on all the prosperity which shall be bestowed upon Israel; and there shall not be an old man in your house for ever. The man of you whom I shall not cut off from my altar shall be spared to weep out his eyes and grieve his heart; and all the increase of your house shall die by the sword of men. And this which shall befall your two sons, Hophni and Phinehas, shall be the sign to you: both of them shall die on the same day. And I will raise up for myself a faithful priest, who shall do according to what is in my heart and in my mind; and I will build him a sure house, and he shall go in and out before my anointed for ever. And every one who is left in your house shall come to implore him for a piece of silver or a loaf of bread, and shall say, 'Put me, I pray you, in one of the priest's places, that I may eat a morsel of bread.'"
(1 Sam.2:27-36 RSV)

This passage shows how a man of God came to Eli the high priest and pronounced judgment on his family because of the wickedness of his children Hophni and Phinehas.

Scripture says that the sons of Eli were wicked men who had no respect for the Lord and treated the Lord's offering with contempt by sending their servants with three-pronged forks to take meat by force from anyone who offered sacrifices to the Lord. Their servants would thrust the fork into the pan, kettle, cauldron, or pot, and the priest would take whatever it brought up. They also slept with the women who served at the entrance to the tent of meeting.

STRATEGIC PRAYER

When Eli their father heard about the wicked things his children were doing, he cautioned them, though they didn't listen to him. Their sin was so serious in the sight of God that he sent a man to pronounce judgment on Eli's family. The word the man of God spoke against the household of Eli ran in his bloodline for over eighty years until it finally blocked everyone in that lineage from being the high priest in the temple.

When Adonijah, the elder brother of Solomon, attempted to make himself king over Israel, he prepared chariots and horsemen with fifty men to run in front of him. He also conferred with Joab, the commander of Israel's army, and Abiathar the priest, and they gave him their support. Then he went to the Stone of Zoheleth, which is by Enrogel, and sacrificed sheep, oxen, and fattened cattle. He invited all his brothers, the king's sons, and all the royal officials of Judah. But he didn't invite Nathan the prophet, Benaiah, the special guard, or Solomon his brother.

When King David called Zadok the priest and Nathan the prophet and Benaiah son of Jehoiada, he said to them, "Take your lord's servant with you and set Solomon my son on my own mule and take him down to Gihon. There have Zadok the priest and Nathan the prophet anoint him king over Israel. Blow the trumpet and shout, 'Long live King Solomon!'"

As soon as Solomon was fully established as king over Israel, he ordered Benaiah son of Jehoiada to execute Adonijah for treason and Joab son of Zeruiah for murdering two commanders of Israel's armies, Abner son of Ner and Amasa son of Jether. However, he did not execute Abiathar the priest for supporting Adonijah, but he dismissed him from his priestly office and put Zadok in his position.

BREAKING TRANSGENERATIONAL CURSES

Abiathar the son of Ahimelech lost his family members because of David when King Saul attacked Nob, the town of the priests, and killed the men, women, children, cattle, donkeys, sheep, and goats, including eighty-five priests who wore priestly garments that Doeg the Edomite killed with the sword by the order of the king (1 Sam.22:6-23).

He (Abiathar) escaped, reported the incident to David, and stayed with him. So he became David's priest and ministered to him in things relating to God. He went through the desert experience with David hoping that when God fulfilled his promises and established him over Israel, he would be the high priest in the Temple that would be built, not knowing there was something running in his bloodline that would disadvantage and disqualify him in the end.

By reason of Abiathar's sacrifices, loyalty, and commitment to David, he should have been the high priest that witnessed the Shekinah glory of God in the magnificent temple Solomon built in Jerusalem, if not for the fact that he supported Adonijah, who attempted to make himself king over Israel. Everyone would think Abiathar lost his position because of the mistake he made by supporting Adonijah, but scripture says it happened to him as a result of the judgment pronounced on his father's house eighty years before him (1 Ki. 2:26 and 27).

Solomon said to him, "Go back to your home in Anathoth. You deserve to die, but I will not kill you now, because you carried the Ark of the Sovereign Lord for David my father and you shared all his hardship."

STRATEGIC PRAYER

So Abiathar lost his office at the time he was supposed to enter his rest and be established as high priest in the Lord's house simply because of what ran in his ancestral root from one generation to another that stood against him and brought him down when he should have been honored.

Many things happen in our lives as a result of what exists and runs in our bloodline that make us repeat history. Trans-generational curses could result in suicide, murder, premature death, jail, pain, tears, misfortune, depression, discouragement, accident, loss, and the like. It is very important to do some background checks and identify incidents or patterns in your ancestral roots and deal with them in prayer, using the appropriate weapons.

CHAPTER 9

PATTERNS OF THE BLOODLINE

There are so many things happening in our lives as a result of what runs in our bloodline, ancestral root, foundation, background, family tree, lineage, line of descent, and so on. These kinds of things cannot be successfully dealt with without addressing the root cause. And to identify the root cause, you have to dig into your family history to find out why certain things happen the way they do.

The Psalmist asks, "If the foundations are destroyed, what can the righteous do?" (Ps.11:3). Many people think that because they are born again, everything about them changed. The truth is that new birth makes us one with Christ by regenerating our spirit man from the spiritual death that came on mankind from the beginning through Adam when he transgressed the commandment of God (1 Co.6:17, Rom.5:18-21).It also saves us from eternal damnation and gives us hope of eternal life in Christ Jesus. But it does not detach us from our family tree.

STRATEGIC PRAYER

2 Corinthians 5:17 says if anyone is in Christ, he is a new creation; the old has gone, the new has come. The reason for this is that the blood of Jesus washes our sins and makes us whole as God imputes his righteousness that is by faith to us at new birth and brings us into the kingdom of his Son.

Colossians 1:12-13 declares that God qualified us to share in the inheritance of the saints, having delivered us from the dominion of darkness, and transferred us to the kingdom of his beloved Son. When God transferred us to the kingdom of his Son, he did not separate us from our bloodline or root. The only change that occurs is that of position, from the kingdom of darkness to that of Christ through the regeneration of our spirit man. However, our mind and character remain the same. This is why scripture admonishes us to renew our minds and change our behavior (Rom.12:2, 2 Co.4:16, Eph.4:23, Col.3:10).

When Lazarus got sick, his sisters sent a messenger to tell Jesus that the one he loved was sick, hoping the Lord would come to heal him so that he wouldn't die. But Jesus remained where he was for two more days before saying to his disciples, "Let us go back to Judea." On his arrival at Bethany, he found that Lazarus had already been in the grave for four days.

When they took Jesus to where they had buried him, the Lord commanded the dead man to come out of the grave and he came forth, his hands and feet bound with linen stripes, and his face wrapped with a cloth around his face (Jn.11:1-44). Jesus said to them, "Loose him, and let him go."

PATTERNS OF THE BLOODLINE

Sickness killed Lazarus, but the traditions and customs of the people bound him. The Jewish custom demanded that when a person died, he should be wrapped with spices in strips of linen before he was buried (Jn.19:40). This is why Lazarus' hands, feet, and face were wrapped with a cloth that prevented him from experiencing total freedom.

Jesus' intervention liberated him from the power of sickness and death, but tradition, custom, and the hand of men bound him. Though Lazarus was liberated by the Lord from what killed him, he wasn't really free because of what ran in his ancestral root and family background. This is what I call *liberated, but not free.*

Just as sickness killed Lazarus, but the tradition of his people bound him, we all died through the sin of Adam, and have been tied up by the traditions and customs of our father's house. When Jesus intervened, he arrested the power of the grave and raised him to life, but instructed those around to loosen the man from the yoke of his tradition so he could go and fulfill his destiny.

Likewise, the death and resurrection of the Lord Jesus redeemed our souls from death and gave us eternal life. For us to enjoy the full benefit of the finished work of Christ on the cross, we must be detached from whatever runs in our bloodline that has bound us up. It could be covenant, curses, customs, traditions, beliefs, altar, sacrifices, and so forth.

Unless we do this and address certain things in our background, faith confession won't take us anywhere. God respects his word and does things in accordance with the principles that he established.

STRATEGIC PRAYER

Just as the Lord Jesus didn't untie the rope that tradition placed on Lazarus, but instructed somebody to do it, God won't do everything for us. He has empowered and gifted some people to help others break out of the restriction that customs, and traditions have put on their lives.

The Lord Jesus said in Matthew 15:6b, "… Thus you nullify the word of God for the sake of your tradition." In accordance with the words of the Lord Jesus in this very passage, we see that our traditions have the ability to negate or annul the word of God in our lives. I think one of the reasons is that God respect principles, and he won't violate the order he established in the beginning regarding earth affairs.

Numbers 30:1-16 describes how much God respects the principles, structure and order he established amongst humans. It says if a young woman makes a vow or pledge to the Lord, under an oath while still living in her father's home, and her father hears about her vow but says nothing to her, then all her vows will stand. But if her father refuses to let her fulfil the vow when he hears about it, all her vows will become invalid; the Lord will forgive her because her father would not let her fulfil them. For the Lord to grant humans such right means he is a God of order and principles.

"When a young woman still living in her father's house makes a vow to the Lord or obligates herself by a pledge and her father hears about her vow or pledge but says nothing to her, then all her vows and every pledge by which she obligated herself will stand. But if her father forbids her when he hears about it, none of her vows or the pledges by which she obligated herself will stand; the Lord will release her because her father has forbidden her.

PATTERNS OF THE BLOODLINE

"If she marries after she makes a vow or after her lips utter a rash promise by which she obligates herself and her husband hears about it but says nothing to her, then her vows or the pledges by which she obligated herself will stand. But if her husband forbids her when he hears about it, he nullifies the vow that obligates her or the rash promise by which she obligates herself, and the Lord will release her. "Any vow or obligation taken by a widow or divorced woman will be binding on her. "If a woman living with her husband makes a vow or obligates herself by a pledge under oath and her husband hears about it but says nothing to her and does not forbid her, then all her vows or the pledges by which she obligated herself will stand. But if her husband nullifies them when he hears about them, then none of the vows or pledges that came from her lips will stand. Her husband has nullified them, and the Lord will release her. Her husband may confirm or nullify any vow she makes or any sworn pledge to deny herself. But if her husband says nothing to her about it from day to day, then he confirms all her vows or the pledges binding on her. He confirms them by saying nothing to her when he hears about them. If, however, he nullifies them some time after he hears about them, then he is responsible for her guilt." These are the regulations the Lord gave Moses concerning relationships between a man and his wife, and between a father and his young daughter still living in his house.
(Num.30:3-16NIV)

If there are things like covenants, curses, customs, traditions, beliefs, altar, sacrifices, etc. running in our bloodline or that our ancestors established before we were born, they could hinder us from enjoying the full benefit of the cross if they are not dealt with.

STRATEGIC PRAYER

Now there was a famine in the days of David for three years, year after year. And David sought the face of the Lord. And the Lord said, "There is bloodguilt on Saul and on his house, because he put the Gibeonites to death." So the king called the Gibeonites and spoke to them. Now the Gibeonites were not of the people of Israel but of the remnant of the Amorites. Although the people of Israel had sworn to spare them, Saul had sought to strike them down in his zeal for the people of Israel and Judah. And David said to the Gibeonites, "What shall I do for you? And how shall I make atonement, that you may bless the heritage of the Lord?" The Gibeonites said to him, "It is not a matter of silver or gold between us and Saul or his house; neither is it for us to put any man to death in Israel." And he said, "What do you say that I shall do for you?" They said to the king, "The man who consumed us and planned to destroy us, so that we should have no place in all the territory of Israel, let seven of his sons be given to us, so that we may hang them before the Lord at Gibeah of Saul, the chosen of the Lord." And the king said, "I will give them."
(2 Sam.21:1-9 ESV)

The passage above gives a clear picture of how your foundation affects you. King David was a man greatly loved by the Lord. In fact, scripture calls him a man after God's heart (1Sam.13:14). During his reign, there was a famine for three successive years, so he inquired of the Lord to know why things were happening that way. God said to him, "It is on account of Saul and his bloodstained house;, because he put the Gibeonites to death."

PATTERNS OF THE BLOODLINE

The Gibeonites were not part of Israel but were survivors of the Amorites that the Israelites had sworn to spare when they took over the land of Canaan. But Saul, in his zeal for Israel and Judah, had tried to destroy them completely from the land.

Joshua 9:3-21 informs us of how the Gibeonites heard about what Joshua did to Jericho and Ai, and they resorted to a trick and sent a delegation whose donkeys were loaded with worn out and old wineskins, cracked and mended. The men wore old clothes and patched sandals, and took dried and moldy bread. When they arrived at the camp of Israel at Gilgal, they told Joshua and the men of Israel that they came from far country to make a peace treaty with them.

When Joshua asked who they were and where they came from, they answered:

Your servants have come from a very distant country because of the fame of the Lord your God. For we have heard reports of him: all that he did in Egypt, and all that he did to the two kings of the Amorites east of the Jordan-Sihon king of Heshbon, and Og king of Bashan, who reigned in Ashtaroth. And our elders and all those living in our country said to us, 'Take provisions for your journey; go and meet them and say to them, "We are your servants; make a treaty with us." ' This bread of ours was warm when we packed it at home on the day we left to come to you. But now see how dry and moldy it is. And these wineskins that we filled were new, but see how cracked they are. And our clothes and sandals are worn out by the very long journey."
(Jos. 9:9-13 NIV)

STRATEGIC PRAYER

The Israelites examined their food, but they did not inquire of the Lord. So Joshua made peace treaty with them to let them live, and the leaders of the people ratified it by oath. After three days, the Israelites heard that the Gibeonites, with whom they had made a peace treaty, lived near them. The whole assembly grumbled against the leaders because of the treaty, but the Israelites could not attack them because of the oath.

The leaders of the assembly said to them, "We have given them our oath by the Lord, the God of Israel, and we cannot touch them now. This is what we will do to them: We will let them live, so that God's wrath will not fall on us for breaking the oath we swore to them."

Many years after the covenant was established with the Gibeonites by Joshua and the leaders of the people of Israel, King Saul broke the agreement in his zeal for Israel and Judah by attacking and killing the Gibeonites in an attempt to annihilate them. When David succeeded him as king over Israel, what King Saul did provoked a famine that lasted three years, which made David to inquire of the Lord.

God told him his situation was due to the action of his predecessor. Then the king summoned the Gibeonites and asked them, "What shall I do for you? How shall I make atonement so that you will bless the Lord's inheritance?" The Gibeonites replied:

We don't want any money from Saul and his family. And it's not up to us to put anyone in Israel to death." But David persisted: "What are you saying I should do for you?" Then they told the king, "The man who tried to get rid of us, who schemed to wipe us off the map of Israel

PATTERNS OF THE BLOODLINE

— well, let seven of his sons be handed over to us to be executed — hanged before God at Gibeah of Saul, the holy mountain." And David agreed, "I'll hand them over to you.
(2 Sam.21:4-6 THE MESSAGE)

The king selected seven males from the lineage of King Saul and handed them over to the Gibeonites, who killed all of them and exposed them on the hill before the Lord.

The same way King David was seriously affected by the actions of his predecessors, despite the fact he was a man after God's own heart, and that he had an everlasting covenant with God, we could be affected by certain actions of our ancestors.

We notice also that nothing worked until king David addressed the foundation and corrected the errors of the one who stood in that office before him. There are voices, powers, covenants, curses, sacrifices, spirits, and the like, controlling and working against us from behind the scenes because of the things that exist in our foundation, and unless we identify those things and deal with them in prayer, the wicked will keep using them to exact on our destinies.

Had King David not sought the face of God to find out why things were falling apart, he would never have located the root cause of his problem. To break out, he had to deal with the problem using the appropriate weapons. Whatever happened in your ancestral root in the past and present affects you directly unless you detach yourself and claim divine exemption by prayer.

When you take a closer look at the life of the Patriarchs, beginning from father Abraham to Jacob, and even to the twelve sons of Israel, you'll observe some patterns that repeated at different times in their lives. Some of the patterns were positive while others were negative.

There are some spiritual and physical things we inherited from our ancestors that make us go through certain things in life. The Bible declares there was a severe famine in the land that made father Abraham to move to Egypt so he could live there for a while. As he approached the border of Egypt, he said to his wife Sarah (Sarai at the time), "Look, you are a very beautiful woman. When the Egyptians see you, they will say, 'This is his wife. Let's kill him; then we can have her!' So please tell them you are my sister. Then they will spare my life and treat me well because of their interest in you." (NLT)

When they finally entered Egypt, the Egyptians saw that Sarai was a very beautiful woman. So the palace officials spoke well of her to Pharaoh and took her to his house. For this reason, Pharaoh treated father Abraham well and gave him many gifts because of her. But the Lord sent terrible diseases on Pharaoh and his household because of Sarai (Gen.12:10-20). Father Abraham lied about his wife Sarah because he was afraid the Egyptians would kill him because of her.

Years later, Abraham moved to Gerar and lived there for a while. Again, he lied about Sarah his wife and said she was his sister. So King Abimelech of Gerar sent for Sarah and took her. But God came to Abimelech at night and told him that the woman he took was a married woman.

PATTERNS OF THE BLOODLINE

However, Abimelech hadn't slept with her yet, so he asked the Lord whether he was going to destroy an innocent nation, given that he did it with a clear conscience, for Abraham told him that Sarah was his sister, and she also confirmed it.

God instructed him to return the woman to her husband, adding that Abraham would pray for him, and he would live, for he was a prophet. But if Abimelech refused to return Sarah to Abraham, he and all that belonged to him would die. So King Abimelech obeyed God and restored Sarah to Abraham as he was instructed (Gen.20:1-18).

In the days of Isaac, the son of Abraham, scripture says there was famine in the land like it was in father Abraham's time. So Isaac took the same steps his father took in his time and he went to Abimelech king of the Philistines in Gerar. God appeared to him there and told him not to go down to Egypt like his father did. So Isaac stayed in Gerar because the Lord instructed him to dwell there, for that is where he would enjoy God's presence and blessing.

When the men of the place asked him about his wife Rebekah, he told them she was his sister because he thought they might kill him on account of her, for she was so beautiful (Gen.26:1-11). One day, Abimelech king of the Philistines looked through the window and saw Isaac caressing Rebekah, so he summoned him and said, "She is really your wife! Why did you say, 'She is my sister'?" Isaac answered him, "Because I thought I might lose my life on account of her." This was the same reason his father Abraham lied about his own wife Sarah.

STRATEGIC PRAYER

The spirit of lying did not stop with Isaac; it affected his children also. Scripture recounts how Jacob lied to his father Isaac to deceive him and get his blessing. When Isaac grew old and his eyes became very dim that he could not see, he called his eldest son Esau and said to him, "I am now an old man and don't know the day of my death. Now then, get your weapons – your quiver and bow – and go out to the open country to hunt some wild game for me. Prepare me the tasty kind of food I like and bring it to me to eat, so that I may give you my blessing before I die."

Rebekah overheard what Isaac told her firstborn Esau. So when the young man left to hunt for the wild game that his father demanded, his mother called Jacob and said to him, "Look, I overheard your father say to your brother Esau, 'Bring me some game and prepare me some tasty food to eat, so that I may give you my blessing in the presence of the Lord before I die.' Now, my son, listen carefully and do what I tell you: Go out to the flock and bring me two choice young goats, so I can prepare some tasty food for your father, just the way he likes it. Then take it to your father to eat, so that he may give you his blessing before he dies."

Jacob followed his mother's advice and brought her the young animal that she used to prepare a very delicious meal, such as Isaac loved. And then she gave it to Jacob to take to his father in order to get his blessing.

She took the best clothes of Esau, her older son, which were with her in the house, and put them on Jacob, her younger son. In addition, she covered his arms and the smooth part of his neck with the skin of the goat that she used to prepare the meal.

PATTERNS OF THE BLOODLINE

Jacob went to his father and pretended to be his brother Esau. Jacob said to his father, "I am Esau your firstborn. I have done as you told me. Please sit up and eat some of my game, so that you may give me your blessings." In the end, Jacob stole his brother Esau's blessing through lies and deception (Gen.27:1-40).

This unfortunate scene reoccurred in the days of Jacob's children. Genesis 37:1-36 relates how the sons of Jacob lied to him about the death of his beloved son Joseph, who they sold to the Ishmaelites for twenty shekels of silver. The passage says Jacob loved Joseph more than any of his other sons because he had borne him in his old age, so he made him a robe of many colors. But his brothers hated him because their father loved him more than the rest of them.

Joseph had dreams and shared them with his brothers; this made them hate him all the more, and they could not speak kind words to him. Sometime later, he had another dream and shared it with his brothers and father. They became very jealous of him, but his father kept the matter in mind.

One day, his brothers went to feed their father's flock near Shechem. So Jacob sent Joseph to go see how they were doing in the field and bring him back a report. When Joseph's brothers saw him in the distance coming to them, they plotted to kill him. "Here comes the dreamer!" they said to each other. "Come now, let's kill him and throw him into one of these cisterns and say that a ferocious animal devoured him. Then we'll see what comes of his dream."

STRATEGIC PRAYER

When he got to where his brothers were, they stripped him of his robe of many colors that he wore and threw him into an empty dry pit. When they saw a caravan of Ishmaelites coming from Gilead, they lifted him out of the dry pit and sold him. They took Joseph's robe and slaughtered a goat and dipped the robe in the blood, and then brought the robe to their father to see whether he would recognize it. They said to him, "This is what we found; please identify whether it is your son's robe or not."

When he looked at it closely, he recognized it and said, "It is my son's robe. A fierce animal has devoured him. Joseph is without doubt torn to pieces." For this reason, Jacob tore his clothes, put on sackcloth, and mourned for his son many days. All his children came to comfort him, but he refused to be comforted. "I will go to the grave mourning for my son," said Jacob as he wept.

This was something that started with father Abraham for fear of being killed on account of his wife Sarah. He lied to Pharaoh and Abimelech to save his life. His son Isaac followed his paths and did exactly what his father did by lying to Abimelech about his wife Rebekah, thinking they might kill him because of her, if they found out that she was his wife. Years later, a situation occurred that made his son Jacob to lie to him in order to steal his elder brother Esau's blessing.

In the days of Jacob, his sons also lied to him about Joseph, his favorite son. Jacob killed a goat, prepared it and used its skin to deceive his father Isaac, but his children killed the same goat and used its blood to deceive him about his son Joseph.

PATTERNS OF THE BLOODLINE

When the whole thing started with father Abraham, it didn't cause him any pain, but years after, lying traveled through his bloodline and caused those after him so much pain, bitterness, frustration, and tears — it became a pattern that negatively affected the generations after him.

Apart from lying, there were other patterns that also affected the Patriarchs. Scripture declares that Sarah was barren, for she had no children (Gen.11:30). Abraham and Sarah had to wait twenty-five years before giving birth to Isaac (Gen.21:2). Sarah was ninety years old, while Abraham was hundred years old when they gave birth to Isaac.

The Bible says in Genesis 25:21 that Isaac prayed to the Lord for his wife Rebekah because she was barren. The Lord answered his prayer and his wife gave birth after twenty years. Isaac married her at the age of forty and had Esau and Jacob at sixty years (Gen. 25:20 and 26).

When Jacob married Rachel, she could not give birth because she was barren (Gen. 29:31). Father Abraham, Isaac, and Jacob had difficulty giving birth because their wives were barren. It took divine intention for the three of them to have children. Barrenness was a pattern that traveled in their bloodline for years and affected three generations.

The second thing I observed is the loss of birthright by the first son. Ishmael was Abraham's firstborn, but he lost the right to Isaac. Esau was Isaac's firstborn, but he too lost it to his brother Jacob. Reuben was Jacob's firstborn, but he lost the birthright to Joseph. Manasseh was Joseph's firstborn; he too lost it to Ephraim.

STRATEGIC PRAYER

When you look at Ishmael, Esau, Reuben, and Manasseh, they represent four generations of people that experienced injustice, loss, pain, frustration, and denial because of a repeated pattern in their bloodline that disadvantaged them. They were all denied their birthrights and refused the benefits of being the firstborn.

According to the law, they all deserved the double portion of their father's properties (Deut. 21:17), but none of them got it because of the patterns of their bloodline. Their younger brothers — Isaac, Jacob, Joseph and Ephraim — enjoyed the rights of the firstborn sons, though they were not firstborn by birth. Their ancestral root, lineage, foundation, line of descent, background, bloodline, family tree, etc. changed the norm and caused them to inherit what belonged to others by right. Any negative occurrence or pattern in your bloodline can be dealt with through prayer.

CHAPTER 10

HOUSEHOLD ENEMY

A household enemy is the enemy within. The Bible declares in Matthew 10:36 that a man's enemies will be the members of his own house. Most people find it very difficult to accept this simple truth expressed in the Bible about household enemies because they can't imagine their friends or family members harming or hurting them. They often suspect outsiders.

Let me ask you some questions, who knows your secrets, fears, concerns, plans, home, work, dreams, visions, and so on? Is it not those you call friends and to whom you tell your secrets?

The Lord Jesus said in Mark 6:4 that a prophet is honored everywhere except in his hometown, among his relatives and in his own family. Could there be something in one's family that fights against the person's honor and glory? Verse 5 says the Lord could not do any miracles in his hometown except that he laid his hands on few sick people and healed them. Why couldn't he do those mighty works he did elsewhere in his family?

STRATEGIC PRAYER

There were things from his home that stood against his glory and caused his people to despise him. And since they didn't believe he could do it, they refused to bring out their sick, which limited the effectiveness of Jesus' ministry.

The enemies within are unfriendly friends, the Judases amongst the twelve, and the wolves in sheep clothing. They are the worst and the most dangerous enemies to deal with because they know who you are, where you live, what you like, how you act, when you go out or come in, your strength and weakness, dreams and fears, ups and downs, and more.

King David was a mighty warrior who could devour anything on his way when he went to the battlefield. According to the estimation of Ahithophel, who was one of the greatest wise men in the Bible and whose counsels were considered as when a person went to inquire of the Lord, said it would take about twelve thousand strong men to take David down (2 Sam.17:1-3).

None of David's adversaries were able to withstand him and his mighty men in battle. He killed a lion, a bear, Goliath, and numerous mighty men in his time. And wherever he turned, he subdued his enemies and conquered their territories. He was so skillful and great in battle that he didn't lose any war.

Nonetheless, scripture informs us that when a messenger came to Jerusalem and told David that the heart of the people of Israel were with his own son Absalom, he said to all his officials who were with him in the palace to hurry out of Jerusalem for fear of being overthrown by Absalom and his men. And when the king heard that his personal counselor, Ahithophel was among the conspirators with Absalom,

HOUSEHOLD ENEMY

fear seized him that he lifted up his voice in prayer and pleaded with God to turn his counsel into foolishness (2 Sam. 15:13-31). What no other king or kingdom was able to do to King David, his son and personal counselor did to him. The Psalmist says,

If an enemy were insulting me, I could endure it; if a foe were raising himself against me, I could hide from him. But it is you, a man like myself, my companion, my close friend, with whom I once enjoyed sweet fellowship as we walked with the throng at the house of God.
(Ps. 55:12-14 NIV)

The Bible talks about Lot, the son of Haran and nephew of father Abraham. When Haran died, Lot was left to the care of his grandfather Terah (Gen.11:27-31), but after some years, Lot's grandfather Terah also died. When God instructed Abraham to leave his native land, relatives, and father's household and go to the land he would show him, Lot followed him.

Genesis 12:5 says that Abram started off as God instructed him taking Sarai his wife, Lot his nephew, and all the possessions they had acquired in Haran for the land of Canaan. The name Lot means covering or veil. Father Abraham had to take him along as he travel from Haran to Canaan because his father (Haran) and grandfather (Terah), with whom who he could have stayed, were both dead, and being Abram's relative, he could not have abandoned him in Haran. So, Lot went legally with Abram based on the ties, links, and relationships that existed between them both through their bloodline, ancestral root, line of descent, family tree, lineage, etc.

Lot accompanied father Abraham from Haran to Canaan, then to Egypt, and then back to Canaan land (Gen.12:1-20). It was lawful for him to live with Abraham because of the death of his father Haran and his grandfather Terah.

STRATEGIC PRAYER

However, the presence of Lot in Abraham's life became an impediment, obstacle, and hindrance to the fulfillment of his prophetic destiny. The spirit of Lot is a familiar spirit that operates legally in people's life based on the covenant, curse, patterns, customs, and traditions that flow in their bloodline.

When the Lord instructed Abram to leave his native land, relatives, and father's family to a new land, he didn't ask him to take Lot along, but Lot was so tied to him that he couldn't leave him behind as he journeyed to Canaan land. The spirit of Lot stands for anything that operates legally in your life and that veils, covers, or obscures your vision, hinders your movement, brings you unnecessary trouble, strife, conflict, contention, and the like. It could be an ancestral curse, covenant, character, mindset, lifestyle, demonic spirit, and so forth.

Lot, who was traveling with Abram, had also become very wealthy with flocks of sheep and goats, herds of cattle, and many tents. But the land could not support both Abram and Lot with all their flocks and herds living so close together. So disputes broke out between the herdsmen of Abram and Lot. (At that time Canaanites and Perizzites were also living in the land.) Finally Abram said to Lot, "Let's not allow this conflict to come between us or our herdsmen. After all, we are close relatives! The whole countryside is open to you. Take your choice of any section of the land you want, and we will separate. If you want the land to the left, then I'll take the land on the right. If you prefer the land on the right, then I'll go to the left." Lot took a long look at the fertile plains of the Jordan Valley in the direction of Zoar. The whole area was well watered everywhere, like the garden of the Lord or the beautiful land of Egypt. (This was before the Lord destroyed Sodom and Gomorrah.) Lot chose for himself the whole Jordan Valley to the east of them.

HOUSEHOLD ENEMY

He went there with his flocks and servants and parted company with his uncle Abram. So Abram settled in the land of Canaan, and Lot moved his tents to a place near Sodom and settled among the cities of the plain. But the people of this area were extremely wicked and constantly sinned against the Lord. After Lot had gone, the Lord said to Abram, "Look as far as you can see in every direction—north and south, east and west. I am giving all this land, as far as you can see, to you and your descendants as a permanent possession. And I will give you so many descendants that, like the dust of the earth, they cannot be counted! Go and walk through the land in every direction, for I am giving it to you."
(Gen.13:5-17 NLT)

The passage above informs us that Lot also became very wealthy with flocks of sheep and goats and herds of cattle and that he had many tents simply because he was traveling with father Abraham. It got to a point where the land could not support both of them dwelling together, for their possessions were so great that they could not stay together. Their individual possessions had become a problem to the other person, and a dispute broke out between them.

Lot became who he was because of the oil and grace on father Abraham's life and because Abraham took him from Haran to Egypt and then to Canaan, but Lot still rose against him at the end of the day. This means that no matter what you do for the enemy within, it will turn against you in the end and cause you much pain.

When father Abraham could not take it anymore because of the strife, conflict, struggle, and quarreling, he requested a separation between him and Lot. Scripture says Lot lifted his eyes and saw that the whole plain of the Jordan was well watered, like the garden of the Lord, like the land of Egypt, and he chose it. He then moved his tent and lived among the cities of the plain, while Abraham dwelled in the land of Canaan.

STRATEGIC PRAYER

As soon as Lot parted from Abraham, God said, "Look around from where you are, to the north and south, to the east and west. All the land that you see I will give to you and your offspring forever. I will make your offspring like the dust of the earth, so that if anyone could count the dust, then your offspring could be counted. Go, walk through the length and breadth of the land, for I am giving it to you." (NIV)

The presence of Lot restricted the border of Abraham's territory, as the land could not support both of them living together.

Second, there was strife and contention in the house because of the operation of the spirit of Lot. Lot's herdsmen quarreled with the herdsmen of father Abraham.

Third, Lot always took what appeared to be the best. Verse 10 and 11 say Lot looked around and saw that the whole plain of the Jordan in the direction of Zoar was well watered like the garden of the Lord, like the land of Egypt, he chose it for himself.

Fourth, Lot blocked Abram from hearing from the Lord, for scripture declares that God spoke to him after Lot had separated from him.

Fifth, "lift up your head and look to the four corners of the earth," said the Lord to father Abraham. This means that Lot had clouded and veiled his sight so that he could not see far, and as long as the spirit was at work in his life, he could not see anything. There was no way he could possess what he couldn't see.

Sixth, the Lord promised to multiply his offspring like the dust of the earth that cannot be counted. Seventh, arise and walk through the length and breadth of the land.

CHAPTER 11

BINDING THE STRONG MAN

Satan is not everywhere at the same time because he is not omnipresent. Only God, the creator of heaven and earth, is omnipresent, omniscient, and omnipotent. What the devil does is to strategically position spirit beings in different territories to promote his agenda and perpetuate havoc in the region.

1 John 5:19 says the whole world is under the control of the evil one. Satan establishes networks and systems that enable him to control things in the world. Scripture calls him the great dragon, also known as ancient serpent, devil, or Satan.

When he rebelled against God, he deceived one-third of the angels and deployed them in battle to take over heaven, but Michael with the remaining two-thirds of the angels engaged the dragon and his angels. The dragon and his angels fought back, but they lost the battle and were forced out of heaven because there was no longer a place for them in heaven (Rev.12:1-12). Verse 12 says, "Therefore rejoice, you heavens and you who dwell in them!

But woe to the earth and the sea, because the devil has gone down to you! He is filled with fury, because he knows that his time is short."

Having lost his place in heaven, he established his kingdom over the earth and positioned his angels at different regions to enforce his agenda. Luke 4:5-7 recounts how the devil showed the Lord all the kingdoms of the world in a moment of time and said to him, "I will give you all their authority and splendor; it has been given to me, and I can give it to anyone I want to."

Since the devil holds the earth on lease through the authority man gave him in the beginning, he rules and reigns over the affairs of the kingdoms of men through the fallen angels that he commissioned and positioned over territory. Demons are territorial. They are assigned to specific region with a mandate and they work through humans to carry out their mission, because no spirit being can legally operate on earth without a body.

Just as God works through us by the Holy Spirit to achieve a specific goal at a particular place and in a specific way, Satan works through humans by assigning them demonic spirits that will use them as vessels to achieve his wicked agenda, depending on their position, social status, and location. Ephesians 6:12 says our fight is not against flesh and blood but against principalities, powers, rulers of darkness, and spiritual wickedness in high places.

Or how can one enter a strong man's house and plunder his goods, unless he first binds the strong man? And then he will plunder his house.
(Matt.12:29 NKJV)

BINDING THE STRONG MAN

Scripture talks about a house in the above passage. This implies a specific location over which the strong man has legitimate authority. It could be his dwelling place or the jurisdiction that he oversees.

In Matthew 12:43-45, the Lord Jesus described how evil spirits work. He said when an evil spirit comes out of a person and goes around seeking a resting place and finds no where to stay, it will say, "I will return to the place I left." And when it comes back and finds the place unoccupied, swept, and put in order, it goes out and takes with it seven other spirits more wicked than itself, and they will all enter the person and live there. The last condition of the person will be worse than the first.

I believe the reason for this is that the spirits will take dominion over the person and control all his actions. Such a spirit becomes the strong man controlling the person's life with the help of other spirits that it invited to make sure nobody comes and drives it out of the person like it happened before. The person becomes its house and all that concerns the individual becomes the properties of the evil spirit.

This could also apply to a region, community, state, nation, or continent. Once their dominion is established over the place through the authority that the person or persons give them, everything in the place comes under their influence and command, and they will take drastic measures to protect and preserve the territory and everything in it. There are several ways by which humans give demonic spirits legal rights and authority over regions, lives, and properties that establish and authorize them to perpetuate their wicked agenda in the place

STRATEGIC PRAYER

When the spirit that controls a nation, state, community, house, or person is demonic, it becomes the strong man over the territory and determines what happens there unless it is bound or cast out of the place. Mark 3:27 says that no one can enter into a strong man's house and take away his possession unless he first binds him.

The six thousand demons that possessed the man at Gerasenes earnestly begged the Lord Jesus not to send them out of the area when he commanded the spirits to leave the man, because the territory was their home and jurisdiction. They even preferred to live in pigs than to be driven out of the region (Mk.5:1-13).

As earlier mentioned, demons are territorial, because their power is regional, and it is determined by the authority the people living in the area give them through certain practices, customs, systems, words, and deeds that open doors and establish legal grounds in the spirit realms for them to operate. Driving them out of the region terminates their authority and operation because it causes them to lose the legitimate right to function in the new territory especially when those living in it don't do any of the things that give demons the authority to operate.

Luke 11:21-22 declares that when a strong man, fully armed, guards his house, his properties are safe. But when someone stronger than he attacks and overpowers him, he strips him of his weapons and carries off his belongings.

By reason of the death and resurrection of the Lord Jesus Christ, the Godhead gave us divine authority to exercise in the name of his Son Jesus. At the mention of the name of Jesus, every knee should bow in heaven, on earth, and beneath the earth, and every tongue should confess that Jesus Christ is Lord, to the glory of the Father (Phi.2:5-11).

You can bind any strong man and overturn their works wherever you live. All you have to do is to learn how to exercise your divine authority in the name of Jesus and deploy the appropriate weapons when dealing with the strong man in your territory, home, school, neighborhood, workplace, city, nation, continent, and so on. You can use any of the techniques we already discussed to analyze things in your area in order to identify the kinds of spirits at work before engaging them in battle to liberate the region from their grip and change the spiritual climate over the area as you take dominion and superimpose God's reign and will over the place.

When Elisha became sick with the illness that he died from, Jehoash king of Israel went down and wept over him and said, "My father, my father, the chariots and horsemen of Israel!" Elisha responded, "Take a bow and arrows." So he got a bow and arrows. Then Elisha said to the king of Israel, "Put your hand on the bow." So the king put his hand on it, and Elisha put his hands on the king's hands. Elisha said, "Open the east window." So he opened it. Elisha said, "Shoot!" So he shot. Then Elisha said, "The Lord's arrow of victory, yes, the arrow of victory over Aram. You are to strike down the Arameans in Aphek until you have put an end to them." Then Elisha said, "Take the arrows!" So he took them. Then Elisha said to the king of Israel, "Strike the ground!" So he struck the ground three times and stopped. The man of God was angry with him and said, "You should have struck the ground five or six times. Then you would have struck down Aram until you had put an end to them, but now you will only strike down Aram three times."

(2 Ki. 13:14-19 HCSB)

CHAPTER 12

DESTROYING DEMONIC ARROWS

Demonic arrows are Satan's weapons of warfare that he uses to engage Christians in battle. Ephesians 6:16 admonishes us to take up the shield of faith, with which we can extinguish all the flaming arrows of the evil one. The wicked use arrows to destroy, kill, afflict, torment, frustrate, scatter, oppress, imprison, hinder, vex, or trouble lives.

Whenever an arrow is shot, it carries some deadly venom or fire that it releases on its target once it touches it. In the old days, bows and arrows were used for diverse purposes such as hunting, fighting, criminal activity, etc. The arrowhead was often coated in the venom of deadly snakes, spiders, or scorpions. Some used them to shoot fire and other deadly substances at people. When the arrow hits its target, the venom or whatever it carried was released to destroy or kill the person or animal.

Similarly, demonic arrows are used by the wicked to release sickness, trouble, disease, untimely death, depression, frustration, manipulation, lost, pain, bitterness, delay, weeping, lack, stagnation, rejection, failure, division, hatred, disappointment on people through witchcraft, enchantment, incantation, divination, sacrifice, spell, curses, and the like. These are deadly arrows fired from satanic covens, altars, evil forests or sacred sites by evil people against families, loved ones, marriages, career, finances, health, destinies, success, businesses, relationships, or the wellbeing of others.

The Bible declares that when Balak the son of Zippor, king of Moab, and all his people saw everything the Israelites did to the Amorites, they were terrified (Num. 22:2-41). So the king of Moab said to the elders of Midian, "This mob will devour everything in sight, like an ox devours grass in the field."

Therefore, he sent messengers to call Balaam son of Beor, who was living in Pethor near the Euphrates River with the following message: "A people has come out of Egypt; they cover the face of the land and have settled next to me. Now come and put a curse on these people, because they are too powerful for me. Perhaps then I will be able to defeat them and drive them out of the country. For I know that those you bless are blessed, and those you curse are cursed."

The elders of Moab and Midian set out with money that they would use to pay Balaam for him to place a curse on the people of Israel. God had to intervene and stop Balaam from doing so. Numbers 22:12 says that God said to Balaam, "Do not go with them. You must not put a curse on those people, because they are blessed."

DESTROYING DEMONIC ARROWS

In the morning, Balaam asked the officials Balak sent to him to go back home, because God refused to let him go with them to the land of Moab and placed a curse on the Israelites.

When Balak noticed this, he sent other officials, more numerous and distinguished than the first ones. They came to Balaam and said to him, "Thus says Balak the son of Zippor: Let nothing stop you from coming to me, because I will reward you handsomely and do whatever you say. Come and put a curse on this people for me." Balaam got up in the morning, saddled his donkey and went with them. This kindled God's anger, and he sent an angel to oppose him.

The angel of the Lord came and stood on Balaam's way with a sword drawn in his hand to kill him. Had it not been for his donkey that saw the angel of the Lord standing in the road with a drawn sword in his hand and turned off the road, the angel would have killed Balaam, because the Lord was angry that he was going to put a curse on his people.

When he finally got to where Balak was staying, both of them went to Kiriath-Huzoth, where the king sacrificed cattle and sheep. In the morning Balak took Balaam to a place where he could see the outskirts of the Israelite camp. There he built seven altars and sacrificed a young bull and a ram on each altar so that Balaam would use it to place a curse on the people of God. But the Lord stepped in and stopped him from cursing his people by putting words that carried blessings in his mouth (Num. 23:1-30).

Curses are demonic arrows that Balak brought Balaam to place on the children of Israel through divination, enchantment, sacrifice, and altars so that the Moabites would defeat the Israelites and drive them out of the land.

And the Lord met Balaam, and put a word in his mouth, and said, "Return to Balak, and thus shall you speak." And he came to him, and, lo, he was standing beside his burnt offering, and the princes of Moab with him. And Balak said to him, "What has the Lord spoken?" And Balaam took up his discourse, and said, "Rise, Balak, and hear; hearken to me, O son of Zippor: God is not man, that he should lie, or a son of man, that he should repent. Has he said, and will he not do it? Or has he spoken, and will he not fulfill it? Behold, I received a command to bless: he has blessed, and I cannot revoke it. He has not beheld misfortune in Jacob; nor has he seen trouble in Israel. The Lord their God is with them, and the shout of a king is among them. God brings them out of Egypt; they have as it were the horns of the wild ox."
(Num. 23:16-22 RSV)

Another passage that clearly depicts how arrows work is 2 Kings 13:14-19. The prophet Elisha had retired from a public ministry that had lasted for about sixty years. It is believed by many Bible scholars that he was possibly over ninety years old when Jehoash, the king of Israel, came to him for help because of the situation he was in at the time.

The passage says the king wept over him. When you see kings crying like babies, you have to understand that they have tried everything within their power to make things work but failed. His military strategy and security intelligence could not help him, and he had to turn to the old sick prophet who had retired from active public ministry for help.

DESTROYING DEMONIC ARROWS

The prophet Elisha inherited the double portion of the spirit of his master Elijah, and he did many mind-blowing miracles in his prophetic ministry. He divided the river Jordan, healed the waters, cursed a group of forty-two that mocked him so that two bears came out of the woods and mauled them. He also multiplied the widow's oil, gave the Shunammite woman a son and raised him to life when he died, healed Naaman's leprosy, made an ax head to float on water, multiplied bread, trapped the blinded Syrian army, and stopped the famine in Samaria. It is believed the prophet Elisha did about thirty-two miracles.

The prophet could have used any other means from his ninety years of experience as one of the greatest prophets that ever lived to help the king who was weeping over him. But the only prophetic direction he gave him was to take a bow and arrow and then shoot it towards the direction of his enemies in order to defeat them.

He said to the king of Israel, "Take a bow and arrows." And the king did as he told him. Then Elisha instructed him to draw the bow as he laid his hand on the king's hands. "Open the eastern window," and he opened it. Then he said, "Shoot!" So he shot an arrow. "This is the Lord's arrow, an arrow of victory over Syria! For you will fight the Syrians in Aphek until you have completely conquered them."

Again he said to the king, "Take the arrows and strike the ground with them." He struck three times and stopped. The man of God was angry with him and said, "You should have struck five or six times, then you would have struck down Syria until it was totally destroyed. Now you will defeat it only three times.

STRATEGIC PRAYER

2 Kings 13:25 says Jehoash recaptured from Ben-hadad the son of Hazael the towns that had been taken from Jehoash's father in war. Jehoash defeated Ben-hadad on three occasions and recovered the cities of Israel just like the prophet said. This is to show you how powerful arrows are.

Now when Elisha had fallen sick with the illness of which he was to die, Joash king of Israel went down to him and wept before him, crying, "My father, my father! The chariots of Israel and its horsemen!" And Elisha said to him, "Take a bow and arrows." So he took a bow and arrows. Then he said to the king of Israel, "Draw the bow," and he drew it. And Elisha laid his hands on the king's hands. And he said, "Open the window eastward," and he opened it. Then Elisha said, "Shoot," and he shot. And he said, "The Lord's arrow of victory, the arrow of victory over Syria! For you shall fight the Syrians in Aphek until you have made an end of them." And he said, "Take the arrows," and he took them. And he said to the king of Israel, "Strike the ground with them." And he struck three times and stopped. Then the man of God was angry with him and said, "You should have struck five or six times; then you would have struck down Syria until you had made an end of it, but now you will strike down Syria only three times."
(2 Ki.13:14-19 ESV)

The arrow that Jehoash the king of Israel shot through the window towards the direction of his enemies was divinely programmed by the prophet Elisha through prophetic decree and declaration to release defeat on the Syrian army. As it flew, it became an arrow of victory to the Israelite but one of defeat, death, shame, and destruction to the Syrian army.

DESTROYING DEMONIC ARROWS

When they met on the battlefield, the Syrians suddenly started losing the fight without knowing why it turned out that way. They gathered courage, changed strategy, and engaged Israel in battle like they used to do, thinking they would win, but they failed again while Israel prevailed against them. They made another attempt to recover their lost ground but could not succeed. They failed three consecutive times because the outcome of the battle was already decided by the prophet Elisha with a bow and arrows from a little room.

In the same way that the prophet Elisha used an arrow to release defeat, loss, and death on the Syrian army through prophetic declarations, the wicked use the same weapon to discharge evil, death, sickness, frustration, depression, hindrance, rejection, lack, accidents, negative incidents, confusion, division, loss, curses, pain, spells, tears, hatred, violence, trouble, distress, suffering, sorrow, misery, and sadness in people's lives through witchcraft, divination, enchantment, incantation, or sacrifice from their secret coven, altars, and sacred sites in order to destroy them. That is why demonic arrows must be blocked, stopped, and caused to misfire and backfire through offensive prayer.

The death of Ahab, the king of Israel, is another event in the Bible that reveals how dangerous arrows are (1 Ki.22:1-38). The king said to his officials, "Do you know that Ramoth-Gilead belongs to us, and we keep quiet and do not take it out of the hand of the king of Syria?"

So he asked Jehoshaphat, the king of Judah, whether he would join him in battle to recover Ramoth-Gilead, which belonged to the tribe of Levi but was under the control of Syria. The king of Judah agreed to join him in the battle against Syria, but he wanted to know whether God approved of the plan.

Ahab gathered four hundred prophets and asked them, "Shall I go to war against Ramoth Gilead, or shall I refrain?" They answered, "Go up, for the Lord will give it into the hand of the king." But Jehoshaphat was not fully convinced by the prophecy. So he asked, "Is there not here another prophet of the Lord of whom we may inquire?" The king of Israel said there was one more person called Micaiah who could consult the Lord for them, but he didn't like the man because he never prophesied anything good about him (the king).

The king later sent an officer to bring the prophet Micaiah so he could tell them the will of God concerning the situation. The messenger who went to get Micaiah said to him, "Look, all the prophets are promising victory for the king. Be sure that you agree with them and promise success." Micaiah said, "As surely as the Lord lives, I will say only what the Lord tells me to say."

When he arrived, the king asked him, "Micaiah, should we go to war against Ramoth-Gilead, or should we hold back? He answered him, "Go up and triumph; the Lord will give it into the hand of the king." But the king insisted that the prophet speak only the truth to him in the name of the Lord. Then Micaiah said, "I saw all Israel scattered on the hills like sheep without shepherd, and the Lord said, 'These people have no master. Let each one go home in peace.'" The king of Israel said to Jehoshaphat, "Did I not tell you he would not prophesy good concerning me, but evil?"

DESTROYING DEMONIC ARROWS

In the end, the king of Israel and Jehoshaphat king of Judah went to Ramoth-Gilead to fight the Syrian armies. King Ahab said to Jehoshaphat, "As we go into battle, I will disguise myself so no one will recognize me, but you wear your royal robes." The king of Israel disguised himself, and they went into battle.

The king of Syria had commanded his thirty-two chariot commanders not to fight or attack anyone else except the king of Israel. When he got to the battlefield, none of the thirty-two commanders recognized him, because he was camouflaged.

Jehoshaphat would think that it was an honor for him to dress in his royal attire, but he didn't realize it was a setup designed to switch his destiny. Had it not been for God who helped him, he would have died in place of King Ahab, because the strategy Ahab employed confused the Syrian army officers who were instructed to kill him and caused them to focus on King Jehoshaphat.

A certain man drew his bow and shot it randomly at the Israelite troops and hit the king of Israel between the joints of his armor. When King Ahab saw that he was seriously wounded by the arrow, he told his chariot driver to get him out of the battlefield. The combat continued all day, and he died that evening.

When King Ahab disguised himself, he became invisible to the thirty-two captains of the Syrian army who were trained and commanded to fish him out and hunt him down. None among the thousands of their soldiers was able to identify Ahab in the battlefield and kill him because he used a tactics that confused all his enemies. At the very moment Ahab thought he had escaped the plot of the enemy, a certain man shot an arrow by chance and hit him so badly that he died the same day.

STRATEGIC PRAYER

We notice in the story that though Ahab appeared invisible to all other weapons the enemies used, he could not dodge the arrow, and as soon as it hit him, he died. This is to show you why demonic arrows should be stopped and destroyed by prayer. They are very dangerous and deadly because of what they carry.

CHAPTER 13

ENFORCING PROPHETIC DECREES

The great apostle Paul instructed his son Timothy in 1 Timothy 1:18 to go to war in accordance with the prophetic words spoken about him. When God speaks, his word does not enforce itself. It has to be enforced by the church, which is God's law enforcement agency on earth.

The apostle knew that for the prophetic words of God concerning his son Timothy to be fulfilled, he had to enforce them through prayer, and not just any kind of prayer, but offensive prayer, because many things would try to negate the fulfillment of the word.

Prophetic decrees are weapons of spiritual warfare used for enforcing God's original will on earth. They give you direction and help you to be in complete alignment with the will, purpose, and counsel of the Lord.

Whenever God reveals his mind, will, counsel, or judicial decision concerning a thing, it must be enforced to ensure full compliance on earth. And the only way to do that is by prayer, because God's kingdom and will cannot manifest in this world without the prayers of the Saints.

STRATEGIC PRAYER

The Bible declares in Psalm 115:16 that the highest heaven belongs to God but the earth he has given to humans. The Lord won't do anything on earth without the cooperation, or authorization from mankind. For this reason, scripture demands that we pray for God's kingdom to come and for his will to be done on earth just as it is in heaven. Nothing happens in heaven outside the will of God because the angels, who are great in strength, ensure the absolute compliance of the heavenly creatures with God's judicial order in heaven by enforcing his words.

Psalm 103:20 declares, "Praise the Lord, you angels, you mighty ones who carry out his plans, listening for each of his commands." (NLT)

As it is written: "I have made you a father of many nations." He is our father in the sight of God, in whom he believed — the God who gives life to the dead and calls things that are not as though they were. (Rom. 4:17 NIV)

The scripture above says God calls things that are not as though they were. When God speaks, no matter how impossible it may look, it will certainly come to pass because his word has the force of law. Nonetheless, it must be enforced by prayer on earth, which is man's domain, to make certain there is thorough compliance.

God's words are the judicial executive order of heaven. The Lord reigns and rules by edict and decree. The angels listen attentively to perform his divine order in heaven. For there to be fulfillment of God's word on earth, humans must enforce it, for God's word will not enforce itself.

ENFORCING PROPHETIC DECREES

The reason many are not experiencing the fulfillment of their prophetic word is because they do nothing about it. There are things you have to do through prayer to activate God's word.

The Bible recounts what King David did as soon as he heard the word of God through the mouth of the prophet Nathan concerning his family. After God had established King David over his people and given him rest from all the surrounding enemies, he purposed in his heart to build a house for the Lord to dwell in. He then summoned the prophet Nathan and shared his plan with him, "Whatever you have in mind, go ahead and do it, for the Lord is with you," the prophet said to King David. That same night, the Lord gave the following word to the prophet for the king:

Go and tell my servant David, 'This is what the Lord has declared: Are you the one to build a house for me to live in? I have never lived in a house, from the day I brought the Israelites out of Egypt until this very day. I have always moved from one place to another with a tent and a Tabernacle as my dwelling. Yet no matter where I have gone with the Israelites, I have never once complained to Israel's tribal leaders, the shepherds of my people Israel. I have never asked them, "Why haven't you built me a beautiful cedar house?"' "Now go and say to my servant David, 'This is what the Lord of Heaven's Armies has declared: I took you from tending sheep in the pasture and selected you to be the leader of my people Israel. I have been with you wherever you have gone, and I have destroyed all your enemies before your eyes. Now I will make your name as famous as anyone who has ever lived on the earth! And I will provide a homeland for my people Israel, planting them in a secure place where they will never be disturbed. Evil nations won't oppress them as they've done in the past, starting from the time I appointed judges to rule my people Israel.

STRATEGIC PRAYER

And I will give you rest from all your enemies. "'Furthermore, the Lord declares that he will make a house for you—a dynasty of kings! For when you die and are buried with your ancestors, I will raise up one of your descendants, your own offspring, and I will make his kingdom strong. He is the one who will build a house—a temple—for my name. And I will secure his royal throne forever. I will be his father, and he will be my son. If he sins, I will correct and discipline him with the rod, like any father would do. But my favor will not be taken from him as I took it from Saul, whom I removed from your sight. Your house and your kingdom will continue before me for all time, and your throne will be secure forever.'" So Nathan went back to David and told him everything the Lord had said in this vision.
(2 Sam. 7:5-17 NLT)

The Bible declares that as soon as David heard this prophetic word, he went straight to the presence of God in prayer and sat before the Lord. In verse 25, the king enforced the prophetic word by saying, "And now, O Lord God, confirm the word that you have spoken concerning your servant and concerning his house, and do as you have spoken." Verse 27 informs us that the reason King David was bold in prayer was because of the word God revealed to him.

As I mentioned earlier, prophetic word is a weapon of spiritual warfare that we use to enforce God's original will and counsel in the earth through prayer because it reveals God's mind, and knowing the purpose of God concerning a thing gives you direction, focus, and boldness in prayer, and it helps you to be in total alignment with God's perfect will in the battleground.

ENFORCING PROPHETIC DECREES

When God instructed the prophet Elijah to go present himself to King Ahab in 1 Kings 18:1 and informed him that he was about to send rain to the land after about three and a half years of severe famine in Israel, Elijah obeyed and did all that the Lord commanded him to do.

He told the king in verse 41 to go get something to eat and drink because he heard the sound of an abundance of rain. This was after he had built an altar in the name of the Lord, made a huge sacrifice (a bull and 12 large jars of water at the time of severe drought), called down fire from heaven, and killed four hundred and fifty prophets of Baal. King Ahab went off to eat and drink, but the prophet Elijah climbed to the top of Mount Carmel, bent down to the ground, and put his face between his knees in an intensive prayer to enforce the prophetic word of God for the land.

Then he sent his servant to go look toward the sea whether he would see the sign of the fulfillment of the prophetic word, and so he went but saw nothing. He came back and told his master Elijah that there was no sign. The prophet Elijah kept praying to enforce and birth the prophecy as he sent his servant to look for a sign. The seventh time, the young man reported to his master that a cloud as small as the size of a man's hand was rising from the sea.

Elijah instructed him to go tell the King Ahab to hurry up and go back home before the rain stopped him (1 Ki.18:1-46). The apostle James says he prayed earnestly to enforce the prophetic word God spoke concerning the land before he could see the fulfillment (Jas.5:17-18).

STRATEGIC PRAYER

When God promised father Abraham that he would give him the land of Canaan to possess, he believed the word of God, and scripture says the Lord credited it to him as righteousness. Then again, he asked, "O Sovereign LORD, how can I know that I will gain possession of it?" At this, God asked him to offer a sacrifice. In the evening, a smoking fire pot with a blazing torch appeared and passed between the pieces of sacrifice. The Bible declares that the Lord made a covenant with Abram that day.

Then the word of the Lord came to him: "This man will not be your heir, but a son coming from your own body will be your heir." He took him outside and said, "Look up at the heavens and count the stars — if indeed you can count them." Then he said to him, "So shall your offspring be." Abram believed the Lord, and he credited it to him as righteousness. He also said to him, "I am the Lord, who brought you out of Ur of the Chaldeans to give you this land to take possession of it." But Abram said, "O Sovereign Lord, how can I know that I will gain possession of it?" So the Lord said to him, "Bring me a heifer, a goat and a ram, each three years old, along with a dove and a young pigeon." Abram brought all these to him, cut them in two and arranged the halves opposite each other; the birds, however, he did not cut in half. Then birds of prey came down on the carcasses, but Abram drove them away. As the sun was setting, Abram fell into a deep sleep, and a thick and dreadful darkness came over him. Then the Lord said to him, "Know for certain that your descendants will be strangers in a country not their own, and they will be enslaved and mistreated four hundred years. But I will punish the nation they serve as slaves, and afterward they will come out with great possessions. You, however, will go to your fathers in peace and be buried at a good old age.

ENFORCING PROPHETIC DECREES

In the fourth generation your descendants will come back here, for the sin of the Amorites has not yet reached its full measure." When the sun had set and darkness had fallen, a smoking fire pot with a blazing torch appeared and passed between the pieces. On that day the Lord made a covenant with Abram and said, "To your descendants I give this land, from the river of Egypt to the great river, the Euphrates — the land of the Kenites, Kenizzites, Kadmonites, Hittites, Perizzites, Rephaites, Amorites, Canaanites, Girgashites and Jebusites."
(Gen.15:4-21 NIV)

Sacrifice carries, activates, and releases the power of a covenant, and it is one of the many things that add weight to prayer in enforcing a prophetic decree. Let me point out here that there is a little difference between a sacrifice and seed faith.

The Bible declares that a seed produces after its kind and that there is seed and harvest time (Gen.1:11-12, 8:22). The Lord gives seed to the sower and bread for food (2 Co. 9:10). The Teacher encourages us in Ecclesiastes 11:6 to sow our seeds in the morning and at evening because we do not know which will produce a harvest. The Psalmist also says that he who goes out in tears to sow his seed will return with songs of joy, carrying sheaves with him (Ps.126:6).

All seeds are not the same, but each seed produces after its kind. When you sow a seed faith for a particular thing, it will produce exactly what you sow. Galatians 6:7 says we reap whatever we sow.

On the other hand, a sacrifice is something precious, special, and valuable that costs you. It is something you go out of your way to offer and when you do, you feel it. It is not just any kind of offering.

STRATEGIC PRAYER

When you look at the Bible closely, you'll notice how specific God is about the kind of animal or things you can offer as sacrifice. And when you do not offer the right thing, the sacrifice will be rejected. But a true sacrifice carries, activates, and releases the power of a covenant. God made a covenant with father Abraham when he offered his sacrifice in the passage we saw earlier.

The Lord says in Psalm 50:5, gather to me all my children who have made a covenant with me by sacrifice. God says in Malachi 1:8 that it is wrong for you to offer a blind, crippled, or diseased animal as sacrifice. This is why a sacrifice must be special, precious, and valuable to move the hand of God.

Apart from sacrificial offerings and seed faith, there are many other things that add weight to your prayer when enforcing prophetic decrees. For more information on this, go to chapter two, under the heading, "Weapons of Spiritual Warfare". You may also go to my other book, *Understanding the Art of prayer (Revisited),* chapter seven, under the heading, "Keys to effective Prayer."

From Genesis to Malachi, there were numerous prophecies about the birth, life, and assignment of the Lord Jesus, but for the word to be fulfilled, people had to stand in prayer and enforce the prophecies. One of them was a prophetess named Anna, the daughter of Phanuel from the tribe of Asher. Her husband died seven years after their marriage. Then she lived as a widow to the age of eighty-four. She never left the temple day or night, fasting and praying to enforce the prophecies concerning the redemption of Jerusalem (Lk.2:36-38).

ENFORCING PROPHETIC DECREES

Another person was Simeon, a devout and righteous man who was eagerly waiting for the consolation of Israel. Scripture declares that the Holy Spirit was upon him, and it was revealed to him that he would not die until he had seen the Lord's Messiah. The Spirit led him to the temple at the time Mary and Joseph came to present the baby to the Lord in accordance with the custom of the Law. He took the child in his arms and praised God for letting him see the fulfillment of his promise to his people Israel (Lk.2:25-35). The Bible also describes how the Lord Jesus prayed earnestly in agony to enforce the prophetic words spoken about him from Genesis to Malachi (Lk.22:39-46).

During those many days the king of Egypt died, and the people of Israel groaned because of their slavery and cried out for help. Their cry for rescue from slavery came up to God. And God heard their groaning, and God remembered his covenant with Abraham, with Isaac, and with Jacob. God saw the people of Israel—and God knew."
(Ex. 2:23-25 NIV)

CHAPTER 14

GROANING IN THE SPIRIT

Groaning in the spirit is the highest dimension of prayer. It occurs when an individual with a heavy burden is deeply moved or stirred up to make a prolonged wordless sound in the Spirit by the help of the Holy Spirit, who gives us the ability to speak in heavenly language. This is the highest dimension of agonizing prayer, and it makes a person cry and wail uncontrollably in the Spirit as a result of the stirring, distress, pain, grief, anguish, or uneasiness from within. It could either be defensive or offensive depending on the case. When it is intercession, it is defensive, but if it happens during spiritual warfare as you engage the enemy, it becomes offensive.

Just as we have different levels of prayer, there are dimensions of strategic prayer. Since intercession and warfare are both strategic, groaning in the Spirit is the highest dimension of strategic prayer. All intercessors and prayer warriors do not operate in the same dimension of prayer. It depends on the knowledge, understanding, skills, and experience one has in the area. The more you know and do, the deeper you go!

STRATEGIC PRAYER

The Free Online Dictionary includes in its definition of groan the following: to voice a deep, inarticulate sound, as of pain, grief, or displeasure: to make a sound expressive of stress or strain: [1] a prolonged stressed dull cry expressive of agony, pain, or disapproval: to (low inarticulate sounds) expressive of pain, grief, disapproval[2] etc.

Groaning in the Spirit moves the hand of God more than any other kind of prayer, because it invokes and enforces the power of covenant (God keeps covenants). Exodus 2:23-25 describes how the Israelites groaned because of their slavery and cried out to God for help. The passage says their cry came up to God and he heard their groaning, which made him remember his covenant with Abraham, Isaac, and Jacob. God looked on his people and was concerned about their situation.

During that long period, the king of Egypt died. The Israelites groaned in their slavery and cried out, and their cry for help because of their slavery went up to God. God heard their groaning and he remembered his covenant with Abraham, with Isaac and with Jacob. So God looked on the Israelites and was concerned about them. (Ex.2:23-25 NIV)

---

1. *Groan. (n.d.) American Heritage® Dictionary of the English Language, Fifth Edition.* (2011). Retrieved April 25 2015 from http://www.thefreedictionary.com/groan

2. *Groan. (n.d.) Collins English – Complete and Unabridged.* (1991, 1994, 1998, 2000, 2003). Retrieved April 25 2015 from http://www.thefreedictionary.com/groan

GROANING IN THE SPIRIT

They groaned because of oppression and affliction, but their groans went up to God and moved him to remember the long-forgotten covenant he made with their ancestors. The power of the covenant that their groaning activated caused God to move to Midian where Moses was tending the flock of Jethro his father-in-law, the priest of Midian, and sent him to go free them from their bondage.

The power of this prayer caused their dream or vision that had not been heard of for about 430 years to come alive. It attracted heaven's attention and provoked divine intervention, which made God find Moses (their deliverer) in Midian, set the bush ablaze (divine orchestration), get his attention, call and send him on the mission to free his people from Egypt (Ex.3:1-10). Had they not groaned, none of the above would have happened.

Now Moses was keeping the flock of his father-in-law, Jethro, the priest of Midian, and he led his flock to the west side of the wilderness and came to Horeb, the mountain of God. And the angel of the Lord appeared to him in a flame of fire out of the midst of a bush. He looked, and behold, the bush was burning, yet it was not consumed. And Moses said, "I will turn aside to see this great sight, why the bush is not burned." When the Lord saw that he turned aside to see, God called to him out of the bush, "Moses, Moses!" And he said, "Here I am." Then he said, "Do not come near; take your sandals off your feet, for the place on which you are standing is holy ground." And he said, "I am the God of your father, the God of Abraham, the God of Isaac, and the God of Jacob." And Moses hid his face, for he was afraid to look at God. Then the Lord said, "I have surely seen the affliction of my people who are in Egypt and have heard their cry because of their taskmasters.

STRATEGIC PRAYER

I know their sufferings, and I have come down to deliver them out of the hand of the Egyptians and to bring them up out of that land to a good and broad land, a land flowing with milk and honey, to the place of the Canaanites, the Hittites, the Amorites, the Perizzites, the Hivites, and the Jebusites. And now, behold, the cry of the people of Israel has come to me, and I have also seen the oppression with which the Egyptians oppress them. Come, I will send you to Pharaoh that you may bring my people, the children of Israel, out of Egypt."
(Ex.3:1-10 ESV)

When we pray in tongues, the Holy Spirit gives us the ability to articulate words in the language of the Spirit also known as the "prayer language." But anytime we groan in the Spirit, the Holy Spirit steps in, and he uses our tongues to declare mysteries that cannot be express in words to God the Father.

Romans 8:26-27 explains how the Holy Spirit helps us in our weakness by interceding for us through wordless groans, because we do not know what we ought to pray for. It says the Father who searches our hearts knows what is in the mind of the Spirit as he groans through us, because he intercedes for us in accordance with the will of God. And since the prayer is in harmony with God's will, the answer is guaranteed. 1 John 5:14 declares that if we ask anything according to his will, he hears us. The reason some don't receive answers to their prayers is that they ask with wrong motives.

Groaning in the Spirit is a prayer that is completely in agreement with the will of God. Therefore, it produces results. I call it the highest dimension of prayer because it carries, activates,

GROANING IN THE SPIRIT

and releases the power of covenant, and once a person attains this level of prayer, he or she births God's agenda and superimposes his will over the kingdom of men and the works of the wicked.

John 11:33-44 recounts what happened when the Lord Jesus got to Bethany after Lazarus had died and was buried. Verse 33 says when the Lord saw Mary weeping and the Jews who had come with her also weeping, he groaned in the spirit and was troubled. Verse 35 clearly states that Jesus wept.

Therefore, when Jesus saw her weeping, and the Jews who came with her weeping, He groaned in the spirit and was troubled. And He said, "Where have you laid him?" They said to Him, "Lord, come and see." Jesus wept. Then the Jews said, "See how He loved him!" And some of them said, "Could not this Man, who opened the eyes of the blind, also have kept this man from dying?" Then Jesus, again groaning in Himself, came to the tomb. It was a cave, and a stone lay against it. Jesus said, "Take away the stone." Martha, the sister of him who was dead, said to Him, "Lord, by this time there is a stench, for he has been dead four days." Jesus said to her, "Did I not say to you that if you would believe you would see the glory of God?" Then they took away the stone from the place where the dead man was lying. And Jesus lifted up His eyes and said, "Father, I thank You that You have heard Me. And I know that You always hear Me, but because of the people who are standing by I said this, that they may believe that You sent Me." Now when He had said these things, He cried with a loud voice, "Lazarus, come forth!" And he who had died came out bound hand and foot with graveclothes, and his face was wrapped with a cloth. Jesus said to them, "Loose him, and let him go."
(Jn.11:33-44 NKJV)

STRATEGIC PRAYER

Before the Lord started groaning, scripture says he saw Mary and those who came with her weeping. This stirred him up and released the burden that caused him to groan in the spirit. Verse 38 says Jesus, once more groaning in himself, arrived at the tomb where Lazarus was buried. It was a cave with a stone rolled across its entrance. "Take away the stone," said Jesus. In verse 41, the Lord looked up and said, "Father, I thank you that you have heard me."

A friend once asked, "Why would Jesus say: 'Father, I thank you that you have heard me,' when there is no place in the passage that says he prayed?" He continued, "Was the act of thanksgiving an expression of his confidence and trust in the Father's ability to grant whatever he desired of him, or was he thanking him for a prayer he did before coming to Bethany?"

In response, I said, "When he groaned in the spirit, that was the highest dimension of prayer." For the Lord to say, "Father, I thank you for hearing me," means that he prayed. Verses 33 and 38 reveal that he groaned in spirit, and groaning is the highest dimension of prayer. This then means that through groaning, he enforced and birthed the prophetic word he said concerning Lazarus' situation in verse 4.

But when Jesus heard about it he said, "Lazarus's sickness will not end in death. No, it happened for the glory of God so that the Son of God will receive glory from this."
(NLT)

IMPORTANT ABBREVIATIONS

Gen..Genesis
Ex. ....Exodus
Lev. ....Leviticus
Num. ....Numbers
Deut. ....Deuteronomy
Josh. ....Joshua
Judg. ....Judges
1Sa. 1Samuel
2Sa. 2Samuel
1Ki. 1Kings
2Ki. ....2 Kings
1Ch. 1Chronicles
2Ch. 2Chronicles
Neh. ....Nehemiah
Esth. ....Esther
Ps. .... Psalms
Pr. ....Proverbs
Ecc. ....Ecclesiastics
SoS... Song of Songs
Is. ....Isaiah
Jer..Jeremiah
Lam. ....Lamentations
Ezek. ....Ezekiel
Dan...Daniel
Hos. ....Hosea
Jon. ....Jonah
Mic. ....Micah
Nah. ....Nahum
Hab. ....Habakkuk
Zeph. ....Zephaniah
Hag. .... Haggai
Zec.. Zechariah

Matt.	Matthew
Mk.	Mark
Lk.	Luke
Jn.	John
Rom.	Romans
1Co.	1Corinthians
2Co.	2Corinthians
Gal.	Galatians
Eph.	Ephesians
Phi.	Philippians
Col.	Colossians
1Thes.	1Thessalonians
2Thes.	2Thessalonians
1Tim.	1Timothy
2Tim.	2Timothy
Heb.	Hebrews
Jas.	James
1Pet.	1Peter
2Pet.	2Peter
1Jn.	1John
2Jn.	2John
3Jn.	3John
Rev.	Revelation

PRAYER OF SALVATION

The gospel message also known as the word of faith, belief and open confession play distinct roles in the salvation process, according to Romans 10:8-10. The word of faith produces the faith we need to please God and be at peace with him (Heb.11:6), believing that God raised Jesus from death causes him to impute his righteousness that is by faith to us (Rom.4:22-25). Confessing the lordship of Jesus makes God to infuse our spirit with his eternal life for rebirth.

Salvation does not come by merely verbalizing the *Sinner's Prayer* without faith in Christ atoning sacrifice that comes from hearing the gospel message, repentance from dead works, and open confession of Jesus Christ as Lord and Savior.

1. Believe in your heart that Christ is the Son of the living God.
2. Believe he died on the cross for your sins and iniquities.
3. Believe that God raised him from the dead after three days for your justification.
4. Believe he is at the right hand of the Father in heaven interceding for you.
5. Believe that only Christ has the legitimate right to give eternal life to humans.
6. Ask him to forgive your sins and wash you by his blood.
7. Openly declare him lord of your life from the depth of your heart.
8. Invite him to come and dwell in you.
9. Ask him to write your name in the book of life.

And this is the testimony: God has given us eternal life, and this life is in his Son. He who has the Son has life; he who does not have the Son of God does not have life. I write these things to you who believe in the name of the Son of God so that you may know that you have eternal life.
(1 Jn. 5:11-14 NIV)

If you confess with your mouth the Lord Jesus and believe in your heart that God has raised Him from the dead, you will be saved. For with the heart one believes unto righteousness, and with the mouth confession is made unto salvation.
(Rom.10:9-10 NKJV)

Salvation is found in no one else, for there is no other name under heaven given to men by which we must be saved.
(Acts 4:12 NIV)

If we confess our sins, He is faithful and righteous to forgive us our sins and to cleanse us from all unrighteousness.
(1Jn.1:9-10 HCSB)

Once you finish reading the above portion of scriptures, you can make the following confession with me from the depth of your heart. Believe it as you speak, and you shall be saved in Jesus name.

Dear Jesus,

I believe that you died on the cross for my sins, and rose on the third day for my justification. You took away my sins, iniquities, infirmities and blotted out the handwriting of ordinances that were against me by your blood. You were bruised for my transgressions, and became a curse for me in order to redeem my soul from death.

I beseech you Lord to come into my life today, and make my heart your dwelling place. I confess you now as my Lord and Savior. Write my name in the book of life, and make me a new person. Thank you Lord Jesus for saving me. Amen

Congratulation!

And Elijah said to Ahab, "Go up, eat and drink, for there is a sound of the rushing of rain." So Ahab went up to eat and to drink. And Elijah went up to the top of Mount Carmel. And he bowed himself down on the earth and put his face between his knees. And he said to his servant, "Go up now, look toward the sea." And he went up and looked and said, "There is nothing." And he said, "Go again," seven times. And at the seventh time he said, "Behold, a little cloud like a man's hand is rising from the sea." And he said, "Go up, say to Ahab, 'Prepare your chariot and go down, lest the rain stop you.'" And in a little while the heavens grew black with clouds and wind, and there was a great rain. And Ahab rode and went to Jezreel.

(1 Ki. 18:41-45 ESV)

Follow me on **f** Caesar Benedo
Email.caesben11@yahoo.com

Dépot Légal N° 9606 du 07 / 09 / 2017
Bibliothèque National Du Bénin, 3ème Trimestre

www.ingramcontent.com/pod-product-compliance
Lightning Source LLC
Chambersburg PA
CBHW061649040426
42446CB00010B/1656